South Africa

South Africa

BY ETTAGALE BLAUER
AND JASON LAURÉ

Enchantment of the World
Second Series

Children's Press®

A Division of Grolier Publishing

NEW YORK   LONDON   HONG KONG   SYDNEY
DANBURY, CONNECTICUT

This book is dedicated to Andrew Boraine,
who took us to Crossroads in 1978,
survived banning under the apartheid government,
and became City Manager of Cape Town under
the ANC government.

Consultant: Deborah Kaspin, Ph.D., Assistant Professor, Yale University, New Haven, Connecticut

Please note: All statistics are as up-to-date as possible at the time of publication.

Library of Congress Cataloging-in-Publication Data

Blauer, Ettagale.
      South Africa / by Ettagale Blauer and Jason Lauré.
      p. cm. — (Enchantment of the world. Second series)
      Includes bibliographical references (p.   ) and index.
Summary: Describes the geography, plants, animals, history, economy, languages,
      religions, sports, arts, and people of a country that shares land borders with
      six nations and surrounds one of them.
      ISBN 0-516-20606-0
      1. South Africa—Juvenile literature. [1. South Africa.] I. Lauré, Jason.
      II. Title. III. Series
      DT1719.B58 1998
      916.8—dc21   97-26014
                                                      CIP
                                                      AC

Acknowledgments

Our thanks to the generous help given us by the individuals listed as well as to the many other South Africans we met who took the time to share their thoughts, give us directions, and help us understand the dynamic changes that have taken place in their country.

We thank Cecil, Izak, and Willem Barnard, Alexa MacNaughton, Sybil Sands, Barry Leitch, Gracious Mgwenya, Tome Tweedy, Dezi Rorich, Angela von Schalwyk, Esther Mchangu, Andrea Kuhn, Alex and Andrew Boraine, Lize Hugo, Bongi, Ruth Motau, Esmaré von Tonder, Sandra Prinsloo, André Vorster, Gordon Oliver, and Eric Miller.

Andrew Boraine in Crossroads squatter camp, Cape Town

Cover photo:
Giraffe feeds on
a tall tree in Kruger
National Park

Contents

Chapter

ONE   A New Nation Emerges **8**

TWO   The Look of the Land........................... **18**

THREE   Wild and Wonderful **29**

FOUR   South Africa Becomes a Nation **34**

FIVE   South Africa Invents a New Government **54**

SIX   The Powerhouse of the African Continent ... **66**

SEVEN   A Land of Many Languages **84**

EIGHT   Spiritual Lives................................. **90**

NINE   Leisure Life **100**

TEN   A Day in the Life of South Africa **116**

View of Table Mountain, Cape Town

Springbok

Timeline **128**

Fast Facts **130**

To Find Out More **135**

Index **136**

Day of Mandela's release from prison

A New Nation Emerges

A unique political process began when Nelson Mandela was released from Victor Verster prison in Cape Town, South Africa, on February 11, 1990. It was the last place he was held during his twenty-seven years of confinement, most of them spent on Robben Island. He immediately took a very public leadership role, appearing at rallies all over the country.

F OR THE FIRST TIME IN all those years, the people of South Africa could see the man who represented his country's terrible struggle for equality. Just four years later, in the elections of April 1994, Nelson Mandela became president of South Africa. The events that took place during those four years changed the face of the nation and its people. The process has quite properly been called "the miracle." In spite of South Africa's legacy of violence and extreme racial oppression, the country proceeded along a lawful path. Elections, which took place every five years under the white minority government, continued on schedule, leading to a black-majority government.

A South African newspaper reports Mandela's freedom in 1990.

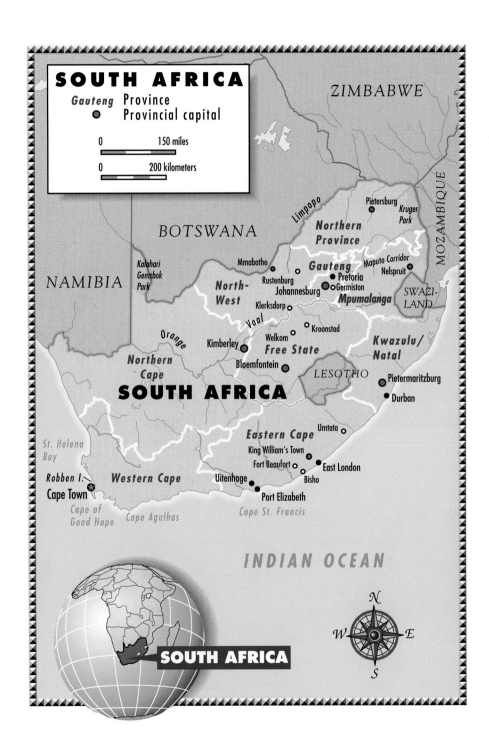

SOUTH AFRICA

Gauteng Province
● Provincial capital

0 _____ 150 miles

0 _____ 200 kilometers

ZIMBABWE

MOZAMBIQUE

BOTSWANA

Limpopo

Pietersburg

Kruger
Park

NAMIBIA

**Northern
Province**

Kalahari
Gemsbok
Park

Mmabatho

Gauteng

Maputo Corridor

Nelspruit

**North-
West**

Rustenburg
Johannesburg

Pretoria
Germiston

Mpumalanga

SWAZI-
LAND

Klerksdorp

Vaal

Kroonstad

Orange

Kimberley

Welkom

**Kwazulu/
Natal**

Free State

**Northern
Cape**

Bloemfontein

LESOTHO

Pietermaritzburg

SOUTH AFRICA

Durban

Umtata

Eastern Cape

St. Helena
Bay

King William's Town

Fort Beaufort

East London

Robben I.

Western Cape

Uitenhage

Bisho

Cape Town

Port Elizabeth

Cape of
Good Hope

Cape Agulhas

Cape St. Francis

INDIAN OCEAN

N

W E

S

SOUTH AFRICA

Geopolitical map
of South Africa

When Nelson Mandela took office on May 10, 1994, most of the people celebrated in the streets. Mandela had achieved his goal: to free his people. The work of creating equality for all the people will take many years. After waiting for generations, many people don't want to wait any more. They want more than the right to have a better life. They want that better life to start today.

Mandela's Fight against Apartheid

Nelson Mandela was imprisoned because he believed that all the people of South Africa, no matter what their color, should be treated equally. But in South Africa, each race group had different rights. The darker their skin color, the fewer rights they had. These decisions were made by the whites who ruled the nation. Whites said people of different races should not live in the same neighborhood, should not go to the same school, should not eat in the same restaurant, and should not marry people of another race.

They believed these things because they misinterpreted certain words they found in the Bible, words they believed told them that blacks were inferior to whites. They did not believe blacks were as smart as whites. They did not believe whites should be forced to mix with people of different colors. These included people originally from India as well as the people who had been created by racial mixing, known in South Africa as "Coloureds."

To make sure of this, they created the policy of apartheid. This is a word in the Afrikaans language and it means "sepa-

During apartheid, blacks and whites were separated even at cultural events.

rateness." Afrikaans is a language spoken by Afrikaners, whites who are descended from Dutch, German, and French who first came to South Africa in 1652. They did not believe that blacks could be educated to the same standards as whites. They could not imagine that people like Nelson Mandela existed. President Mandela is well educated. Although he was born in a rural area and is the son of a chief, he went to university and then studied law. He speaks English and Xhosa, the African language he learned at home as a child. He also speaks Afrikaans, which he learned during his imprisonment.

When President Mandela was born, blacks were not allowed to live in South Africa's cities, which were reserved for white people. Blacks could come to the city during the day to work, but they had to live in townships, places that were set aside for them. These places did not have electricity or running water; they did not have toilets inside the houses.

Townships are located away from the city center and are not easy to reach. Blacks could use only "black" buses and trains. They could be arrested if they were found in a city at night. They had to carry a passbook to prove they had a right to be in the city at all. Thousands of men and women were put in prison for violating the pass laws. Many white people thought black people were undesirable as neighbors or friends. Black people were only supposed to appear when their labor was needed. When they were too old or no work was available, they were supposed to leave the cities entirely and move to poor rural areas called "homelands."

This is the system that Nelson Mandela and

The "separateness" of apartheid

Blacks in South Africa had to carry passbooks.

Oliver Tambo (left) was among the people who fought to end apartheid. Chris Hani (right) was assassinated on April 10, 1993, after years living underground.

political groups organized by blacks were trying to change. Fighting for these changes was against the law. Nelson Mandela, Oliver Tambo, Walter Sisulu, Robert Sobukwe, and thousands of others risked their lives to change these laws. It was a long, dangerous process. For some, such as Thabo Mbeki and Oliver Tambo, it meant living outside the country, as exiles, and fighting for equality. For others, like Chris Hani, it meant living "underground," trying to stay out of sight of the police.

Many died during the years of the struggle for equality and many others grew old in prison. All the people sacrificed part of their lives to gain simple human rights. Today, blacks, Coloureds, Asians, and whites have the same legal rights in South Africa. They can live anywhere they can afford. They can ride in any bus and eat in any restaurant. They can marry anyone they choose. And they can vote for the men and women who govern them. In 1994, when all South Africans were allowed to vote for the first time, they chose Nelson Mandela as their president.

Now that apartheid has ended, South Africa is rebuilding.

But the struggle continues. South Africa must create many new jobs. They must change their school systems so everyone has a chance for a good education. They must find housing for millions of people who live in shacks. It's a tremendous job, and it has become even more difficult as people discover that gaining freedom does not solve all their problems.

Under apartheid, the government controlled everything that affected people's lives. The end of white domination brought an end to most of those controls. Millions of illegal immigrants, many from neighboring Mozambique, flooded into the country. Many of them, and many legal citizens, turned to crime because there was so little work to be found. The new, black-ruled government must put back some of the controls so people feel safe in their own country.

Children of all races now attend school together.

Schools after Apartheid

The change in the rules about where children may go to school and what they are taught has been among the most dramatic and successful in the country's short history as a true democracy. Parents rushed to put their children in better schools and that usually meant formerly white schools. The teaching was better, the books and equipment were better, even the school buildings were better. Even though the law now says that all children learn the same subjects, the level of teaching is not the same. There are not enough well-trained teachers to reach all the black students, especially in the rural areas. But for black, Coloured, and Asian children who live in the cities, going to a better school usually just means traveling farther away from home. It's a trip they're delighted to take.

Integration of the schools was remarkably peaceful, especially considering how hard the white government fought to keep the races apart in education. A few exceptions included the small town of Potgietersrus, about 150 miles (240 km) north of Johannesburg. There, white parents tried to keep blacks out of the white school by first blocking the doors and then by moving the white children to another building. By the end, the parents were forced to give up the struggle and about two dozen black children joined four hundred white children in the primary school.

Higher education has been the privilege of the very few in South Africa, particularly for blacks. The old system set up separate universities for English-speaking whites, for Afrikaners, for Coloureds, for Asians, and for blacks. Now, these universities are open to all races, but there are few places and too many young people trying to enroll. Whites find themselves being passed by in favor of blacks even though many blacks have to take special courses to make up for the poor education they received in the lower grades.

CHAPTER

two

The Look of
the Land

The Republic of South Africa is a land of dramatic
coastlines formed by the Atlantic Ocean to the west
and the Indian Ocean to the east and south. Violent
ocean currents send waves crashing against the rocks
along the shore.

Cape Town

CAPE TOWN, SOUTH AFRICA'S MOST BEAUTIFUL CITY, AND the capital, sits on the edge of the land, with Table Mountain rising up beyond it. Saw-toothed mountains rise up in the east, telling of a great ancient upheaval of the earth. South Africa stretches across the entire width of the African continent. The Cape of Good Hope is considered the very tip of the country but the oceans actually meet at Cape Agulhas, along the southern coast of the country. At this point the cold Atlantic Ocean waters merge with the warm Indian Ocean currents.

Cape Town

Opposite:
View of Table Mountain

The Cape of Good Hope juts into the Atlantic Ocean and was the goal of early explorers.

South Africa's coastline runs for 2,700 miles (4,500 km) and forms three of the nation's borders. There are few natural harbors. The currents and winds that sweep the oceans around the country often make traveling by ship a deadly affair.

The Cape of Good Hope is the dominant feature along the country's coastline and was the major landmark for explorers. It is a nature reserve and the most visited site in the country.

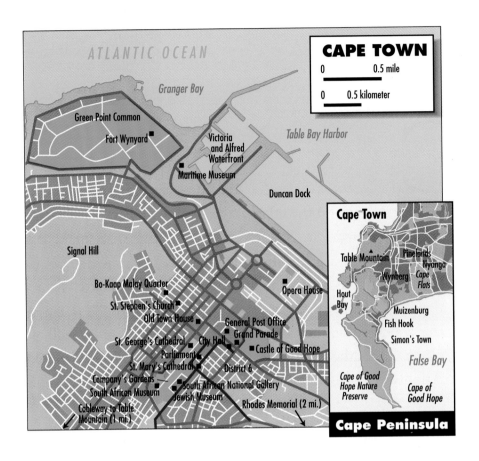

Geographical Features

Area: 472,281 square miles (1,223,201 sq km)

Highest Elevation: Mt. Injasuti 11,181 feet (3,408 m)

Lowest Elevation: Sea level along coast

Longest River: Orange River, 1,300 miles (2,100 km)

Largest City: Johannesburg

South Africa shares borders with six nations. One small country, Lesotho, is surrounded by South Africa. In the north are Botswana and Zimbabwe. To the northwest is Namibia. Most of South Africa's eastern border is shared with Mozambique. Tiny Swaziland is in the northeast.

A Land of Contrasts

Within its land area of 472,281 square miles (1,223,201 sq km), South Africa includes regions of extreme dryness, tremendous rainfall, and fierce winds. These different climates influence how and where people live. Dramatic differences in climate occur wherever mountain ranges create natural barriers to wind and moisture. These natural landmarks run from north to south, about 50 to 200 miles (80 to 322 km) inland all along the coasts, sometimes marching right up to the sea.

Much of the center of the country is a high, dry plateau where little rain falls. Few people live in this region that

The Great Karoo

Topographical map of South Africa

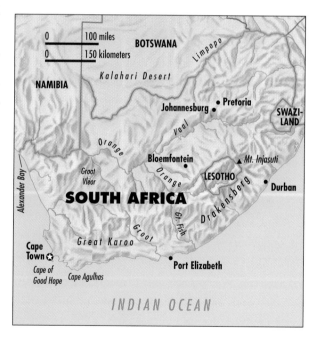

Table Mountain Reserve

Table Mountain is a massive mountain that forms a natural background for the port city of Cape Town. It rises 3,563 feet (1,086 m) above sea level, and then ends abruptly with a flat top. Constant wind and water erosion of the soft sandstone layers created the unusual tabletop. The mountain dominates the Cape of Good Hope peninsula and may be seen up to one hundred miles out at sea. When weather conditions are just right, beautiful white clouds form over the top of the mountain, spill down the face, and then evaporate at the point where the temperature changes. This cloud is called the tablecloth on Table Mountain.

The mountain is part of a chain that runs down to Cape Point, the very tip of the African continent. This region is a distinct zone of plants and flowers, unlike any other in the world thanks to the moisture provided by the "tablecloth." More than 1,470 species of plants are found on the mountain. Wild animals used to roam these cliffs but now only goats and small, furry rock hyraxes are found scampering over the rocks.

A cable car runs to the top of Table Mountain (top left). As the car makes the spectacular ride to the top, all of Cape Town and the harbor come into view. From the top, visitors can see Robben Island, 5 miles (8 km) offshore. Nelson Mandela was imprisoned here for eighteen of the twenty-seven years he spent in jail. Robben Island takes its name from the Dutch word for seals, which once were the island's only residents.

Although Table Mountain Reserve (top right) is a national park, parts of it are privately owned. These owners want to build house and hotels along the lower slopes. Schoolchildren made posters (right) and wrote letters to President Mandela. They asked him to help them save the mountain. "Save the mountain" was the theme of their posters.

stretches from the Great Karoo northward up to the desert regions that form the border with Botswana and Namibia. Karoo is a word in the Bushmen language that means "a great thirstland." It is home to sparsely settled groups of people and to farmers who need vast ranch lands to browse their sheep.

Bushmen paintings can still be found on the walls of Drakensberg caves.

The dramatic peaks of the Drakensberg mountain range

At the eastern end of South Africa, inland from the Indian Ocean, is the Drakensberg mountain range, the highest in southern Africa. The name means "dragon mountains" in Afrikaans. These massive peaks form dramatic valleys where sparkling streams make their way downhill. The earliest people to live here left behind thousands of cave paintings. The Bushmen, also known as the San, painted scenes of hunting and ceremonial dances. These paintings may still be seen.

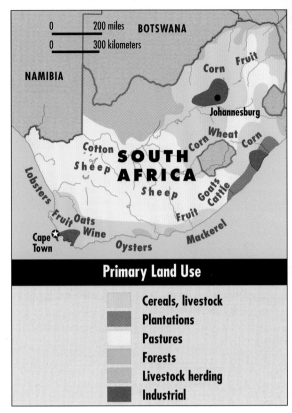

Primary Land Use

- Cereals, livestock
- Plantations
- Pastures
- Forests
- Livestock herding
- Industrial

The Zulu–British Battlefields

The battlefields of the 1879 war between the Zulus and the British lie to the north of the Drakensbergs. Those battlefield sites look very much the same today. Rorke's Drift marks one of the battles of Isandhlwana, where the Zulus defeated the British, a great disgrace in British history. A drift is a low-lying place covered with a shallow stream. The site was named for a British officer. The Zulus, the largest ethnic group in South Africa, number about eight million.

Durban

The city of Durban (top), South Africa's largest port and third-largest city, is a blend of cultures. More than a third of South Africa's million Asian Indians live in the area. This popular beach resort on the Indian Ocean has a subtropical climate. Although it is uncomfortably hot and humid in the summer, Durban's warm and pleasant winters make it a magnet for people from Johannesburg and Pretoria. The city was founded in 1835 on the site of the old Port Natal and was named for Sir Benjamin D'Urban, a British general and governor of the Cape Colony.

The population has changed since the end of apartheid. The Zulus, once restricted to black townships outside the city, have flooded into the central district, crowding out the Asians. Both groups outnumber the whites who once dominated the city. Zulus fill Durban's sidewalks (left), selling crafts to the tourists who stay in the big beachfront hotels along the city's "Golden Mile."

Johannesburg

Johannesburg (top left), South Africa's business center, sits on a plateau more than 1 mile (1.6 km) above sea level. The Zulus call it E'goli', the place of gold, because it was built on top of the gold mines that gave the country its great wealth. In Xhosa, it's called Gauteng.

The central city, is a mix of modern skyscrapers and apartment buildings. Most of the people who work in Johannesburg come from the residential regions that ring the city. As many as six million people live in and around Johannesburg including an estimated two million who live in Soweto, South Africa's biggest black township. Its name comes from the words "south west township." To the north lie the formerly white suburbs, now open to all races but still mainly the home of well-to-do whites.

Although apartheid has ended, most blacks still live in the townships in small "matchbox" houses, many without running water and some without electricity (top right). But many people flooding into the cities live in far worse conditions. They build shacks on any open piece of land they can find. These provide basic shelter so these people are not what we would call homeless. Every day, about one thousand more people arrive at the edges of the city, where they build shacks and try to find work. This shifting population has changed Johannesburg from a white city into a bustling African city. Because of the vast number of unemployed people, crime has made the region into a dangerous place. Many businesses have moved out of the inner city to the northern suburbs.

Mountains of earth taken from the gold mines underneath the city were left behind after the mining process. These "mine dumps" dotted the skyline as the city grew up around the mines. Now they are being reworked to remove tiny bits of gold left behind by the old gold recovery process. Slowly, the dumps are disappearing, and with them, a piece of Johannesburg's history.

The South African spring brings colorful wildflowers.

Vasco da Gama

Vasco da Gama

About five million Zulus live in the area now known as the province of KwaZulu-Natal. KwaZulu means "place of the Zulu people." Natal was named by the Portuguese explorer Vasco da Gama, who first saw the region on Christmas day in 1497. Natal means "birth" in Portuguese.

South Africa's western coastline, stretching northwards all the way to the Namibian border, is an eerie place. Here, icy winds blowing off the Atlantic Ocean meet hot desert air. Few people live in this desolate region that seems lifeless. But every spring, the land blossoms with wildflowers. For a few weeks, the earth is carpeted in blazing color.

Wild and Wonderful

South Africa's wide variety of climate and terrain is home to a dazzling number of plants and animals, many of them unique to the country. The best known and largest wildlife reserves are located in the eastern part of the country. Under apartheid, this great natural resource was enjoyed almost exclusively by whites. Now, although they are open to all, few blacks have their own cars, necessary to tour the parks.

THE PARKS ARE CAREFULLY CONTROLLED AND MANAGED. Visitors drive along paved roads in their own cars. It's illegal to go off the road and drive over the land to look for animals. This careful control has made South Africa one of the most successful countries in animal conservation. If it were not for the country's efforts to take care of certain species such as the rhino, this species would probably be extinct today. Some of these rhinos are sent to other parks now.

South Africa's national flower, the protea, is part of the fynbos family, a floral kingdom unique to the Cape region. In all the world, there are only six floral kingdoms. The protea group of flowers have an exotic look: the spiky-petal flower heads can grow as large as 1 foot (.3 m) across.

The protea, South Africa's national flower

Flora and Fauna

South Africa is the only country where you can see the biggest mammals on land and in the sea. All of the world's thirty-nine whale species can be seen during the migrating season, from September to November, along the coast about an hour's drive from Cape Town.

The Springbok

The springbok, a small member of the antelope family, is unique to South Africa. Its ability to leap far and high made it a perfect choice as the symbol of South Africa's sports teams. To be a springbok champion means you have reached the highest rung in your sport.

When apartheid ended, some people thought the symbol of the country should be changed simply because it was associated with the old South Africa. But when President Mandela appeared at the Rugby World Cup final held in South Africa in 1995 and congratulated the winning South African captain wearing a green springbok jersey, it was official: the springbok symbol was here to stay.

Sabie River

One of many varieties of flowers in Kruger

Kruger National Park

Imagine a wildlife park that's the same size as the entire country of Israel, a park that's 50 miles (80 km) wide and 200 miles (322 km) long. That's Kruger National Park, big enough to hold 7,500 elephants and 2,000 lions (above). Those are not estimates: the game rangers in Kruger know exactly how many animals they have because they keep such careful track of them. Visitors to this vast area travel through fourteen different ecological areas, including forests and plains that are home to different species of wildlife and birds.

Kruger's entire eastern border lies next to the country of Mozambique. Because there was a long civil war in Mozambique, the park officials erected an electrified

fence. It was meant to keep out the people who were fighting and to keep in the animals. During the war, animals straying over the border were likely to be killed for food.

Great size isn't needed to do excellent conservation work. Hluhluwe-Umfolozi Game Reserve, a tiny park in KwaZulu-Natal, is credited with saving the white rhino from extinction. (Hluhluwe-Umfolozi is pronounced "shoosh-louie uhm-fuh-low-zee.") The reserve was once the hunting ground of Zulu King Shaka. The first wilderness trail in the reserve was created by Ian Player and Magqubu Ntombela.

South Africa Becomes a Nation

The written history of South Africa began around 1488, when the Portuguese explorer Bartolomeu Dias first visited the southern coast on one of his voyages of discovery.

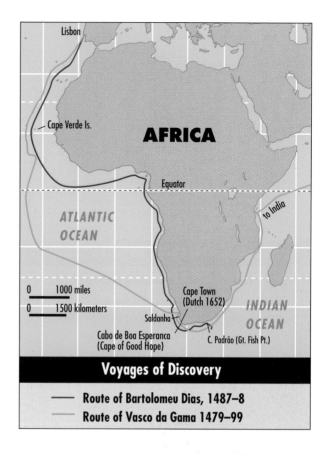

Lisbon

Cape Verde Is.

AFRICA

Equator

to India

ATLANTIC
OCEAN

0   1000 miles
0   1500 kilometers

Cape Town
(Dutch 1652)

INDIAN
OCEAN

Saldanha

Cabo de Boa Esperanca
(Cape of Good Hope)

C. Padrão (Gt. Fish Pt.)

Voyages of Discovery

— **Route of Bartolomeu Dias, 1487–8**
— **Route of Vasco da Gama 1479–99**

Aₗₜₕₒᵤgₕ Pₒᵣₜᵤgᵤₑₛₑ ₑₓₚₗₒᵣₑᵣₛ

LTHOUGH PORTUGUESE EXPLORERS as well as English and Dutch sailors had contact with the local people of southern Africa throughout the next hundred and fifty years, the first white settlement came in 1652 with the arrival of a ship belonging to the Dutch East India Company. Its captain, Jan van Riebeeck, was sent out from Holland to establish a food supply stop for the Company's ships as they made their way around the Cape of Good Hope. He and his men created gardens to grow desperately needed vegetables. This garden may still be seen in Cape Town, in back of the Houses of Parliament, although now only flowers are grown there.

Close contact between the whites and the native people was inevitable. Most of the Dutch men had come without wives, and they sought out the women they found in the Cape. The result was mixed-race children, known in South Africa as "Coloureds." They are considered a distinct race, separate from both black and white.

Shortly after they arrived, the Dutch were joined by Huguenots who had left France to find religious freedom.

Jan van Riebeeck

Opposite: **Cape Town water-front and Table Mountain**

South Africa Becomes a Nation   **35**

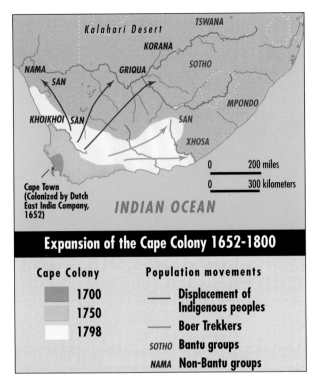

Kalahari Desert

TSWANA

KORANA

SOTHO

NAMA

SAN

GRIQUA

MPONDO

KHOIKHOI SAN

SAN

XHOSA

Cape Town
(Colonized by Dutch
East India Company,
1652)

INDIAN OCEAN

0   200 miles

0   300 kilometers

Expansion of the Cape Colony 1652-1800

Cape Colony	Population movements
1700	—— Displacement of Indigenous peoples
1750	—— Boer Trekkers
1798	SOTHO Bantu groups
	NAMA Non-Bantu groups

Together, these two European groups began to create a new language that would be known as Afrikaans. They called themselves "Afrikaners," people of Africa. They were also known as "Boers," the Dutch word for farmers.

White Population Grows

As the white population at the Cape grew, the settlement began to spread into the interior. When they needed more land, they simply took it. The Boers wanted to be left on their own. They

Jan van Riebeeck

Jan van Riebeeck is the man who was most responsible for establishing a white presence at the southern tip of Africa. He changed the region by creating a society in which race was the dominant feature.

Van Riebeeck and his men began trading with the people who lived in the region. They provided him with cattle, sheep, and goats in exchange for metal products and tobacco. The people were the Khoikhoi and the San, a distinct race of people of small stature and lighter color skin who lived off the land. They gathered wild roots and berries and hunted the wildlife that flourished throughout

the region before white people came. The Khoikhoi also raised domestic animals.

Van Riebeeck began work on a fort, to protect his men and his wife and son, who came with him on the three-month-long voyage from Holland. After five years, nine of the men left the Company to set up on their own. The Company gave land used by the Khoikhoi to these men.

This was the first time native people in South Africa became trespassers in their own land. By this time, blacks had been brought to the area as slaves because the Khoikhoi would not do the hard labor demanded by the Dutch.

didn't want anyone to tell them how to live or how to treat the black and Coloured workers on their farms.

In the late 1770s, as the Boers trekked farther inland, and to the east, they encountered the Xhosa people. The Xhosa and other Africans lived in organized communities and were ruled by traditional chiefs. Many battles took place between the Boers and the Xhosa.

In the meantime, Cape Town had grown into a busy seaport, an appealing target for other Europeans. The British, who were eager to protect their trade routes, set sail for the Cape. In 1795, the British took over the Cape community, with the approval of the Dutch

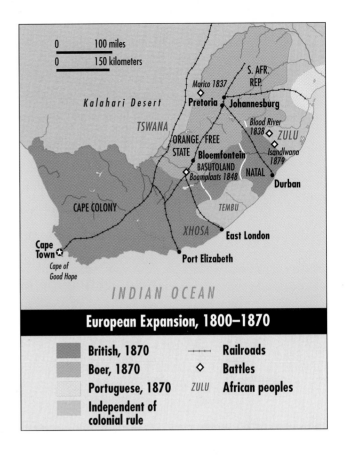

European Expansion, 1800–1870

	British, 1870		------	Railroads
	Boer, 1870	◇	Battles
	Portuguese, 1870	ZULU	African peoples
	Independent of colonial rule		

The busy seaport of Cape Town in 1849

Crown. In 1802, the British signed a treaty giving up the Cape, but four years later, they took the Cape back from the Dutch government, who put up little resistance.

The first group of British to settle at the Cape was very small. They were followed by a larger group known as the 1820 Settlers who formed the base of the English-speaking population. The British and Dutch continued to fight over differences in language and culture. Meanwhile, the Boers were fighting the black African tribes. And the black tribes were fighting each other. All of these groups were seeking land and the right to rule over that land.

Shaka Leads the Zulus

By the beginning of the 1800s, the Zulu people were living in the region of South Africa near the Indian Ocean. These lands were too small for the rapidly growing populations and warfare erupted between different factions. The chiefs concentrated on building up armies of warriors to protect their territories.

In 1815, Shaka (left) came to power as chief of his people. He quickly built up his army to a force of two thousand highly disciplined warriors. Shaka was a brilliant military man. He devised a new method of fighting with a short, stabbing spear called an *assegai*. At the same time he arranged his armies into formations that surrounded the enemy. Using these two ideas, Shaka defeated other tribal groups. The women were taken in and made part of the Zulu people. The Zulu kingdom grew into the largest in all of southern Africa. Shaka ruled for just thirteen years. In 1828, he was killed by his half-brother, Dingaan. But Shaka's influence on South Africa is still felt in Zululand. The Zulus are proud of their warrior history.

The Great Trek

In the 1830s, a group of Boers decided to trek far away from the Cape. They hated being ruled by the British, but the last straw was on December 1, 1834, when the British outlawed slavery. To get away from these laws, they trekked over the Drakensberg Mountains, loading their household goods on ox-drawn wagons. This Great Trek brought them up against the Zulus, the most determined people and the fiercest fighters they had ever encountered. The Boers and the Zulus fought many battles during the early 1800s. The Zulus, with their superior strategy and discipline, under their leader Dingaan, surprised many groups of Boers who were spreading out over the countryside.

One battle is remembered by both sides for its savagery. Andries Pretorius, a Boer leader, took his men into battle at the Ncome River. On December 16, 1838, about five hundred well-armed Boers slaughtered three thousand Zulus. The river ran red with torrents of Zulu blood and since that day the Boers call it Blood River.

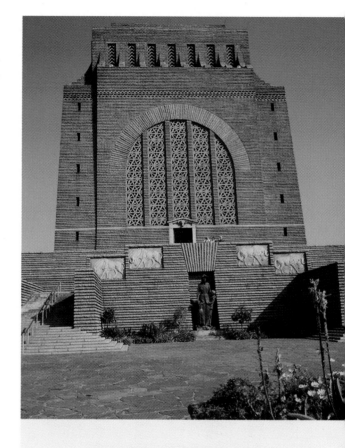

Voortrekker Monument

According to Afrikaner history, when the Boers won the battle of Blood River, they made a vow to God. More than one hundred years later, in 1947, they kept their promise to honor the day. The spot they chose was a hilltop in the city of Pretoria, named for their leader, Andries Pretorius.

The Voortrekker Monument is a sturdy and solemn looking building, designed with an opening at the top. Each year, on December 16, exactly at noon, the sun's rays pass through that opening and strike a plaque inside the building. The battle itself is portrayed all around the monument. This is the holiest shrine of the Afrikaner people.

The Big Hole at Kimberley

The Afrikaners established three independent states that were joined in 1860 to form the South Africa Republic. But the Republic had financial problems from the start and the Afrikaners soon lost control of it.

There was more than politics at stake. The land the Afrikaners had finally settled on after all their trekking holds South Africa's greatest mineral wealth. Diamonds were discovered in 1867, near the Orange River, the heart of the Afrikaners' farming area. This led to the first rush of diggers hoping to strike it rich. In 1871, gold was found in the eastern Transvaal, whose name means "across the Vaal River." It was a small gold strike but it was enough for the British. In order to profit, they had to be in control. In 1877, the British annexed the South Africa Republic and made it part of the Cape Colony.

Cecil Rhodes

Cecil Rhodes had a dream. He wanted the British to control all of Africa "from the Cape to Cairo" and build a railroad to run the length of the continent. He also had a knack for making money. These two qualities helped to change the history of South Africa and the world.

Rhodes was a sick youth, too sick to attend college. Instead, he went to South Africa, where the climate was better than in England. In 1871, he began buying up small mining claims in the diamond mining town of Kimberley. Rhodes and a partner then formed De Beers Consolidated Mines. It was named for De Beers' farm, one of the first places where diamonds were found.

Within twenty years, Rhodes controlled most of the diamond mining industry and had an important stake in gold mining. In 1890, the British government named him Governor of the Cape Colony. Groote Schuur, the piece of land he bought to live on, has been turned into a beautiful park and memorial high above Cape Town.

Although many of Rhodes's dreams did not come true, he left behind a brilliant legacy. In his will, he established scholarships at Oxford University in England for young men from the British colonies and from the United States. President Bill Clinton was a Rhodes scholar from 1968 to 1970.

Conflict over Land and Minerals

Conflicts continued as each group—British, Boer, Zulu, and Xhosa—fought for the same land. The British push into the region known as the Eastern Cape came at the expense of the Xhosa. For more than two hundred years the Xhosa had lived on great stretches of land in the Eastern Cape. Conflict between the British settlers and the Xhosa grew when drought forced the Xhosa to look for new grazing lands for their cattle, lands then claimed by the British. The Xhosa took cattle from the settlers and burned down their homesteads. The British responded by waging war against the Xhosa.

A series of wars between the two sides grew more and more violent. Thousands of Xhosa were killed and more than fifty thousand of their cattle were taken by the British. This became known as the cattle-killing disaster of the 1850s. More than one-third of all the Xhosa died of starvation when they lost both their cattle and their lands.

The disputes over land continued as precious minerals were found in South Africa. The more valuable the land, the more the whites were determined to take it from the blacks.

The biggest gold deposit was found in 1886 on a farm called Langlaagte. The region was called the Witwatersrand, which means "ridge of white waters." Gold and diamonds shaped the future of South Africa. They made a few men very rich and turned hundreds of thousands of others into migrant workers.

The Africans who lived on land near the new mining claims were pushed off that land through a series of legal and illegal maneuvers. It was the stated goal of Cecil Rhodes to deprive the Africans of land so that they would have to turn to the mines for work.

This didn't profit the Boers. They had little money to invest and wanted nothing to do with the English speakers. As the British moved to take firmer control of the land and the people who lived on it, the Boers felt they were being pushed to the very edge of existence.

The British were used to conquering people of color who they thought were not intelligent or "civilized." Now, they set out to conquer a group of whites who they also thought were not civilized. The British looked upon the Boers as poor

Anglo-Boer War

The Anglo-Boer War began in 1899. It followed many smaller battles between the British and the Boers. The war raged on and off until 1902. By the time it was over, the British had brought in 448,000 soldiers, an extraordinary number, five times the number of Afrikaners who fought. The Boers knew the land, and they could count on supplies from the entire Afrikaner community. The British had to transport their men from thousands of miles away and supply them in the field.

The Africans had no direct part in this war that raged all around them. The whites were fighting on land that had once been theirs. About one hundred thousand Africans played some role in the war, as cooks and porters. But no matter which white group won the war, there would be no rewards for the Africans.

While the men fought on the battlefield, about 136,000 Afrikaner women and children were being rounded up and herded into concentration camps. About 115,000 African also were put into camps to keep them from helping the Boers. Conditions were terrible. At least 14,000 blacks and 28,000 whites died of disease and starvation in the camps.

The war dragged on. Some Afrikaners wanted to fight until not one Afrikaner was left standing but the Boers' leaders finally agreed to peace talks. On May 31, 1902, a peace treaty was signed in Pretoria.

farmers who were keeping them from a fortune in gold.

After the British conquered the Afrikaners on the battlefield, they agreed to many of the Afrikaners' most important demands, particularly the recognition of their language.

The black Africans were the real losers in this war. Even though the Boers had lost the war, the British agreed to one of their key demands. Blacks were denied the vote. Laws were passed denying many rights to blacks and also to Indians, who lived mainly in Natal.

Union of South Africa

In 1910, the Union of South Africa was proclaimed. It united the Orange River Colony, the Cape Colony, the Transvaal, and Natal. The exclusion of blacks from any role in the Union

Union Day in Cape Town

led them to create an organization in 1912 that became known as the African National Congress. The future of South Africa was forecast in 1913 when the rulers created the Natives' Land Act. This divided South Africa into "white" and "black" areas, with most of the land set aside for the small white population.

The cities of the new Union were declared "white." Only blacks with jobs could enter the cities. And they were not allowed to live in the cities. Instead, they were confined to crowded black townships outside the city limits. In 1936, land distribution was finalized: whites had given themselves 87 percent of the land. Blacks, who outnumbered the whites by seven to one, were left with 13 percent of the land. Their land was the least useful, the worst for growing crops. As soon as the land act was passed, white farmers began evicting black tenants. Overnight, most of the nation was made homeless.

The struggle between the English speakers and the Afrikaners continued. The Afrikaners were intent on denying blacks any rights, but they did not control the government. The worldwide economic depression of the 1930s reduced many whites to poverty. When World War II began, South Africa sided with the Allies, against the Germans. Many Afrikaners supported the Germans and were opposed to this

During apartheid, blacks and whites had to use separate transportation.

Sharpeville Massacre

Resistance to white domination was continuous but unsuccessful. The South African police and the army were called out every time blacks rose up against the apartheid laws that made their lives so miserable. On March 21, 1960, a group of unarmed blacks made their way to the police station in Sharpeville (a black township) to hold a peaceful protest against the passbook laws (right). No black in South Africa could travel, live, or work without a passbook. This hated document was the record of a person's life as defined by the white government. Thousands of demonstrators left their passbooks at home, expecting to be arrested. They thought this would show the government's policy could not continue if it had to arrest thousands. But the peaceful demonstration was met with gunfire. When it was over, sixty-nine blacks were dead, shot in the back by the police as they tried to flee when the shooting began (top). Their deaths sparked a nationwide protest.

move. Shortly after the war, the Afrikaners got the chance to turn South Africa into the country they always wanted. In 1948, the Afrikaners' National Party won the national election. With absolute control over the nation, they started to put their racial ideas into action.

Apartheid Laws Enacted

They enacted a series of laws that became known as "apartheid." This was the policy of absolute segregation of the races. It stated where a black person could live, go to school, and get medical care and work, and whom that person could marry. It established "homelands" where blacks were supposed to live when they were not working for the whites.

For the next forty-five years, the National Party tightened its control over the lives of blacks, Indians, and Coloureds. Blacks had to carry passes to prove they had a job and a legal right to be in a city or a township. Blacks without jobs, even temporarily, were supposed to go "home" to a homeland, even if they had never seen those places.

The white government, under Prime Minister Hendrik Verwoerd, looked to Britain to support its apartheid policy. Instead, in a February 1960 speech by British Prime Minister Harold Macmillan, in Cape Town, he spoke out against racism. He spoke of "winds of change sweeping over the continent," winds that would sweep out the colonial powers and see the African colonies gain their independence.

Verwoerd, called the architect of apartheid, was in office from 1958 until he was assassinated in 1966. He was notorious

for two policies: "Bantu" education and creation of the "homelands." He claimed black Africans were not South Africans at all but were citizens of these homelands. Verwoerd himself was born in Holland.

An October 1989 march in support of the African National Congress in Johannesburg

The ANC and the PAC

The African National Congress (ANC) and the Pan Africanist Congress (PAC) organized more black resistance to apartheid's laws. As these demonstrations grew in strength, the government grew even more determined to stamp out all protest. On April 8, 1960, the government banned the ANC and the PAC. It became a crime to be a member of these organizations. In response, their leaders went underground. Many world governments, including Great Britain, condemned South Africa's actions. South Africa was still a member of the British Commonwealth of Nations, a group of former colonies with ties to England. Refusing to change its policies, on May 31, 1961, South Africa cut its last ties with Great Britain and declared itself a republic.

The tide of resentment grew as the National Party government moved to enforce the apartheid laws even more strictly. The government forced millions of blacks to move from their homes to fulfill the policy of racial separation. Black leaders had few choices and all of them were dangerous. They could resist apartheid through organizations such as the ANC, or they could escape from South Africa and work for change from outside.

Both paths were followed by some of South Africa's best-educated blacks, people who were not considered worthy of citizenship by the white government. Those who tried to work for change inside the country were either jailed or banned. Blacks were more likely to be jailed; whites were more likely to be banned. Banning was a form of punishment that prevented a person from meeting with more than one person at a time. In practice, it meant not being able to work, sometimes not even being able to eat dinner with your family if there was more than one other adult present. A person who was sentenced to "house arrest" became his or her own jailer.

District Six

Forced removals meant the end of a normal way of life for the victims. Wherever the government saw people of color living in an area now called "white," those people were thrown out. They were sent to distant places without running water or land to farm. In Johannesburg, the lively area known as Sophiatown was emptied of its residents. The houses, bars, and nightclubs where the black writers gathered were all torn down to make way for the white suburb of Triomf (which means "triumph" in Afrikaans).

Then in 1966, the government turned its attention to District Six, in the very heart of Cape Town. District Six was close to the City Hall, close to Parliament, close to the city's business center. Every day, the ministers and members of parliament saw how the people of District Six defied the whole idea of apartheid. The residents were of all races and religions, living in harmony. Most were Coloureds, but there were blacks and whites as well. The government declared the District "white." Shortly after the declaration, soldiers came in the middle of the night and removed the blacks who were living there. Neighbors woke up the next day and found empty houses and apartments where those people had lived. The Coloureds were next to go.

Throughout the 1970s, after numerous threats and warnings failed to work, the authorities simply used force to turn District Six "white." People were tossed out of their houses with their furniture and belongings. Some were taken by truck to remote sites on the Cape Flats, divided according to their race. Others were left on the sidewalk with nowhere to go and no way to get there.

When the people were removed from one block of houses, the bulldozers moved in and reduced the houses to rubble. The idea was to build new houses for white people. The shame of what had been done was so great that no decent white person was willing to live there. The empty streets remained empty. One school, a technical college, was built. But no houses were built (below). That is how District Six remains today, as an empty symbol of apartheid.

Steve Biko served as president of the South African Students Organization.

The second group, those who fled the country, are known as the exiles. They include some of the nation's most important leaders of today, including deputy president Thabo Mbeki. These leaders slipped over borders at night and often traveled far from South Africa where there was financial support and backing for their struggle. Some lived outside the country for nearly thirty years.

Many more left the country because they saw no future there. Elizabeth Furse was a teenager who marched against apartheid with her mother. She came to the United States, became a citizen in 1972, and is now a member of the House of Representatives from Oregon.

Steve Biko

South Africa lurched from crisis to crisis in the years after Sharpeville. In 1968, students founded the South African Students Organization (SASO), with Steve Biko as president. This is considered the beginning of the Black Consciousness Movement. Unlike the ANC, this group did not accept whites as members. They believed that only blacks could fight for their own liberation. Whites, even sympathetic whites, benefited from apartheid.

The government continued to crack down on blacks. In 1976, black students rose up in fury against a new government policy. In a country where so many different languages are spoken, one language must be chosen for students who reach high

school. The students wanted to continue to be taught in English, a language in general use. The government, however, insisted they be taught in Afrikaans, the language the students associated with apartheid. They staged a protest march, in Soweto, on June 16, 1976. Thousands of students boycotted classes and took to the streets of the black township near Johannesburg.

South African police used guns against blacks armed with stones.

The army was called out to put down the protest. The soldiers were ordered to fire at the crowd. Students were shot to death. Even as they tried to get away, the police shot them in the back. It is estimated that one thousand young people were killed. In response, students burned down their own schools. It was the end of education and the start of a new era of oppression in South Africa. Young black leaders rose up to take the place of those in jail but their efforts were stopped at every turn. Steve Biko was brutally murdered by the police while he was being held in detention in 1977.

P. W. Botha

P. W. Botha

Protests continued as the white government changed hands in 1978. The new prime minister, named by the whites, was P. W. Botha. His plan was to eliminate some of the minor apartheid laws such as "whites-only" entrances to building and repealing the laws that prohibited marriage between whites and blacks.

But these changes didn't address the real issue of equality. Meanwhile, white-ruled countries bordering South Africa gained their own independence, starting with Rhodesia, which became Zimbabwe in 1980. This gave hope to the blacks and put even more pressure on the white government.

In 1986, the South African government renewed a State of Emergency that was first declared in 1985. This gave it even more power to detain people on almost any charge. As more whites protested against apartheid, they, too, were imprisoned, banned, and tortured. Still the government held on to its belief that the basic structure of apartheid must be pursued, no matter what the cost.

Finally, though, the cost actually became too great. Governments, including the United States, applied economic sanctions against South Africa. Investments dried up. Corporations withdrew their businesses. South Africa found itself barred from the economic business of much of the world. Athletes from South Africa were not allowed to take part in international competitions such as the Olympics.

de Klerk Ends Apartheid

When President Botha announced that Coloureds and Asians would have their own representatives in Parliament, but blacks would not, rioting broke out in the black townships. The people were outraged that they still had no voice in government. It looked as if the violence would continue as long as Botha was president. Then in 1989, he became ill and was forced to resign. He was replaced by F. W. de Klerk.

President F. W. (Frederik Willem) de Klerk

Former President F. W. (Frederik Willem) de Klerk is an Afrikaner who has a secure place in the history books. He will be remembered as the man who released Nelson Mandela from prison. To most South Africans, including many Afrikaners, this was an honorable decision. The most conservative Afrikaners, however, see him as a traitor.

When he began his political career as a member of South Africa's parliament in 1972, Mr. de Klerk was a loyal member of the National Party who supported the laws against blacks' rights. He rose to a cabinet position in 1978 and was chosen to succeed President Botha in 1989.

Privately, Mr. de Klerk had been thinking about South Africa's future. South Africa had become a police state. The only policy was to continue to rule through force. The country's economy was sinking lower and lower. He believed that apartheid would have to end or the country could not survive. There would be no future for the country's children. The only way to end apartheid was to talk with the leaders of the ANC. He made the decision to unban the ANC. Mr. de Klerk started the remarkable changes that led to Nelson Mandela becoming president.

As soon as he took office, President de Klerk began the real process of ending apartheid. On October 10, 1989, he released important prisoners, including Walter Sisulu, to test the reaction of the people. And then he asked Nelson Mandela to be brought to him from prison for a meeting at the official state president's residence on December 13, 1989. Organizations representing blacks were now allowed to exist. And on February 11, 1990, Nelson Mandela was released from prison. South Africa was ready to enter the modern era. Many obstacles blocked its path. How many whites would support this decision? President de Klerk decided to find out. On March 17, 1992, he held a referendum, a vote on a single question. He asked the whites, "Do you want us to continue the process of ending white rule in South Africa?" The answer was YES! By a margin of more than two to one, 68.7 percent of the voters agreed that this was the right course.

President F. W. de Klerk, who began the process of ending apartheid

South Africa Invents a New Government

The end of apartheid in South Africa meant more than an end to legal racial injustice. A new form of government had to be created. South Africa was a brand-new country, even though it was more than three hundred years old. The people could decide exactly the kind of a country they wanted South Africa to be. It was a unique opportunity and they took full advantage of it.

B
ETWEEN 1990 AND 1993, A TEM-
porary constitution gave blacks full
citizenship. In April 1994, everyone
knew a black man was going to
be elected president. First, though,
blacks and everyone else in the country who was at least eighteen years old
had to be given the right to vote.

Although half of the people in
South Africa cannot read or write,
they can still take part in the political
process. In the first democratic election, millions of people
voted for the first time in their lives. These included people
who were well educated and well respected. It also included
millions of people in the rural and urban areas who lived in
poverty, without electricity or run-
ning water. All of them could vote
and nearly twenty million turned out
to vote. People waited in the hot sun
for hours, some of them all day, to cast
that first ballot. The lines stretched
for miles in some places. The voting
was scheduled to take three days.

In 1994, millions of South
Africans voted for the first
time.

Many voters stood in long
lines to cast their ballots.

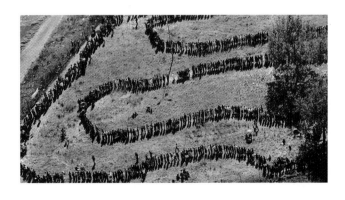

Opposite: **President Mandela
in his African-style shirt**

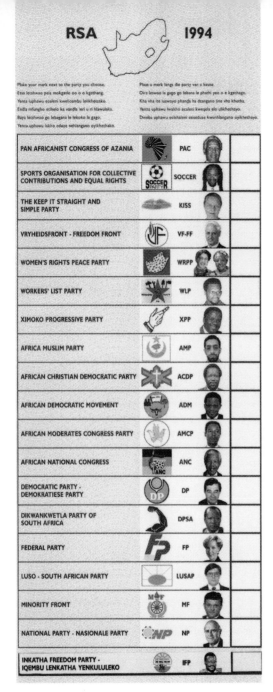

A ballot from the 1994 election

At the last minute, an extra day was added to be sure everyone who wanted to could vote. In the end, 19,533,498 valid votes were recorded.

Black Majority Triumphs

On May 10, 1994, the new government was inaugurated and went to work. Most of the new members of the government were black men and women. Many of them had to learn how to do their new jobs. There were tutors to teach members of Parliament how to enact laws and run the country.

The major task before the legislators was to write a new constitution and to do it within two years. The group chosen, the Constitutional Assembly, faced a tough job. Although the country had changed dramatically, many of the people still clung to old ideas. The committee looked at constitutions used by countries all over the world. They took the parts they liked the best from each and then added many new ideas of their own.

One of the most important parts is the Bill of Rights, an idea taken from the U.S. Constitution. The rights guaranteed by the South African constitution go far beyond those in the United States. They include the right to a healthy environment, housing, health

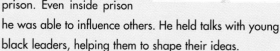

Mandela's Struggle

Nelson Mandela triumphed over South Africa's apartheid system but it took most of his life to break free. He was born in 1918 in a small village in the Transkei. Although the village had no running water or electricity, Mandela was the son of a chief. He was meant to inherit his father's title. Instead, he chose to study law at the University of Fort Hare. He moved to Johannesburg, where he shared a law office with Oliver Tambo in Johannesburg in the 1940s. Most of his cases involved blacks who had broken the pass laws. He joined the African National Congress (ANC) and hoped to overturn those unjust laws. Soon, the police were after him. He was considered a traitor to the country because he spoke out against those laws. His most serious crime, in the eyes of the white government, was declaring that all South Africans should be treated equally, no matter what their color.

When he was put on trial he was able to speak out in public. He explained the ANC's decision to use violence to force changes in South Africa. "We felt that without violence, there would be no way open to the African people to succeed in their struggle against the principal of white supremacy." He stated his beliefs at the trial. "South Africa belongs to all the people who live in it, and not to one group, be it black or white. I have carried the ideal of a democratic and free society in which all persons live together in harmony and with equal opportunity. It is an ideal which I hope to live for and to achieve. But, if needs be, it is an ideal for which I am prepared to die." The government considered him to have committed an act of treason.

With that, the court sentenced him to imprisonment for life. He became South Africa's most famous prisoner. For twenty-seven-and-a-half years he remained in prison. Even inside prison he was able to influence others. He held talks with young black leaders, helping them to shape their ideas.

When he was released from prison he made a remarkably fast entry into life as a citizen. He had not had the freedom to travel, to be with friends, or even to choose what to eat. The rest of the country had been in a kind of prison as well during those twenty-seven years. In spite of changes that had taken place in South Africa, thousands of people were still being arrested simply because they were the "wrong color" in a certain place. Just four years after his release, Nelson Mandela was elected president of South Africa. It is considered one of the most remarkable turnarounds in world politics.

Mandela's cell in Robben Island

Mandela signed the new constitution into law on December 10, 1996.

care, food and water, and education. It protects against discrimination because of sexual orientation. The guarantee of rights does not mean that they will be granted quickly. It does mean that the government is committed to the goal of providing all those rights to all citizens. It is the first time South Africa ever considered all its people to be citizens equally deserving of those rights.

President Mandela signed the new constitution into law on December 10, 1996, at Sharpeville. He chose that place as a way of honoring a pledge to guarantee personal freedom for all South Africans.

Parliamentary Government

South Africa is governed according to a parliamentary system. Parliament is based in Cape Town and has two houses, the National Assembly and the National Council of Provinces. This is a checks-and-balances system, similar to the U.S. Senate and House of Representatives. The head of state is the president who serves a five-year term and is chosen by the members of Parliament. Because the ANC had the majority of votes, 62 percent, they had the biggest voice in choosing the president in 1994. Anyone over the age of eighteen is eligible to vote and to run for office.

The Parliament building in Cape Town

Zulu People

The Zulu people are the single largest ethnic group in South Africa. They number between eight and nine million, about 20 percent of the entire population. During the apartheid years, the government tried to force the homeland of KwaZulu to become an independent country, as part of the grand plan of apartheid. The leader they chose was Mangosuthu Buthelezi (opposite page). While he agreed to be the leader of the Zulus, Mr. Buthelezi refused to accept independence for KwaZulu (home of the Zulus). Instead, he walked a delicate path between the white government, which paid his salary, and the Zulus, who did not want to be restricted to the lands set aside for them. Because it was illegal for blacks to form a political party, Mr. Buthelezi took an old cultural group called Inkatha and turned it into a power base. He is the son of a chief and is known throughout the country as Chief Buthelezi.

During apartheid, he ruled KwaZulu for nearly twenty years. He was the best known black leader not in prison. He had plenty of money to spend, thanks to the white government. When Nelson Mandela was released from prison, the people turned to him for leadership. Even though political parties were legal, and Inkatha became a powerful political force, Chief Buthelezi's power shrunk almost overnight.

He began fighting for his political future. He took the money the government had given to him to run the province and used it instead to stage huge rallies. Thousands of Zulu men and women were bused in to these rallies, carrying their spears and fighting sticks.

Seeing his power slipping away, he pushed the Zulu people into a frenzy of violence. Fifteen thousand Zulu people were murdered between the time Nelson Mandela began negotiating with the white government until the 1994 election. No one could seem to stop the horrible killings that were taking place every week in the hills of KwaZulu.

Then Buthelezi staged a march in downtown Johannesburg, right past the headquarters of the ANC on March 18, 1994, just five weeks before the election. Thousands of Zulus stormed through the streets carrying their weapons. On orders from Nelson Mandela, president of the ANC, guards fired on the marchers from the rooftop of the building, killing eight.

Buthelezi stirred up a different kind of trouble when he declared that he and his Inkatha political party would not take part in the elections. If such a big group boycotted the elections, they would not be accepted as free and fair by the outside world. Instead of voting, Buthelezi talked about pulling his province out of South Africa entirely.

Then, one week before the election, he changed his mind and allowed Inkatha to take part. He saw that even the death of so many Zulus was not going to stop the election process. Millions of ballots had already been printed. Election workers had to paste a new strip of paper onto every single ballot so Inkatha would be included. When the counting was over, the ANC won 62 percent of the vote nationwide. Inkatha received a majority of the vote in KwaZulu-Natal but only 10 percent nationwide. That was enough to secure a Cabinet position for Chief Buthelezi. He was named Minister of Home Affairs.

In spite of this, when the local elections were contested the next year, the murders in KwaZulu began again. Security conditions were so bad, the local elections had to be delayed in that one province. But Buthelezi, who likes to push things as far as possible, saw that he wasn't getting anywhere and once again he called a halt to the violence. He began to carry out his duties as a minister. President Mandela, who believes in reconciliation whenever possible, even named Buthelezi as acting president on occasions when both he and Deputy President Mbeki were out of the country. This would give him the recognition he so desperately wanted. In the western Cape, home of most of South Africa's Coloureds, the National Party won a majority of the vote. This was a shock for everyone, including the Coloureds. Why, after so many years of being treated as third-rate citizens by the National Party, did the Coloureds vote for the party of apartheid? The answer is one that bothers blacks, whites, and Coloureds: the Coloureds thought that life for them would be worse under a black government than it was under the white government. The ANC won the majority of the votes in the other seven provinces.

The premier of each of the nine provinces oversees a legislature that passes laws for that province. These laws must not conflict with national laws. The elected members of the provincial legislatures choose the premiers.

In addition to national, provincial, and local leaders, South Africa also recognizes traditional leaders. These are men and women who are chiefs of their communities. In the past, they were the only figures of authority. They upheld the laws of their people and had absolute authority over their lives. They decided punishment for crimes, they allocated land, and they made treaties with other tribes. Their authority was based on "customary" law, the law of the tribe. The new South Africa constitution recognizes their roles and allows them to act on matters that affect their own community. The traditional leader of the Zulu people is King Goodwill Zwelethini.

AWB leader Eugene Terre'Blanche (center) brutally attacked blacks and tried to stop the election process.

White Opposition

Not everyone was happy with the country South Africa had become. While most whites accepted the changes, and some even welcomed them, one group of Afrikaners, known as the AWB, continued to protest. Led by Eugene Terre'Blanche, they tried to stop the entire process leading to elections and majority rule. Terre'Blanche, whose name means

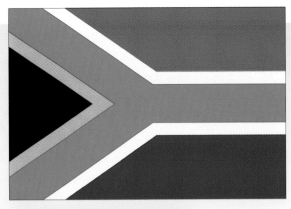

South Africa's Flag

The new South African flag combines red, black, white, green, blue, and yellow in a geometric design. The flag design omits symbols entirely but the colors themselves have meaning. The black, green, and yellow were popular with most of the groups fighting for liberation, while the red, white, and blue appeared on most flags from the colonial and settler periods.

It replaced a flag that had been used since 1927. That flag combined the colors and symbols of the nation's history. It showed the British Union Jack and the flags of two of the former Boer republics, within three bands of color — orange, white, and blue. It reflected the origins of many of the whites but it did not represent the blacks at all. It was a powerful symbol of the white nation.

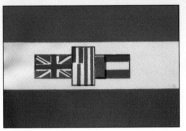

"white earth" in French, organized a small force of Afrikaners. During the negotiating process leading to the temporary constitution, they ran a vehicle right through the plate glass window of the building where the talks were taking place. They tried to start a civil war in the former homeland of Bophuthatswana to show that South Africa could not be governed by blacks. When three AWB members were shot to death there, the armed attacks came to an end. But they continued to demand a "white homeland" so they could live their lives away from the black people.

On December 15, 1993, just four months before the first democratic elections, the AWB held an all-day and -night rally at the Voortrekker Monument. Women, men, and children all took part. They dressed up in nineteenth-century clothes,

National Anthem

In 1897, a Xhosa teacher named Enoch Sontonga wrote a song called "Nkosi Sikelel' iAfrika," ("God Bless Africa"). It became the anthem of the African National Congress. In 1994, when all South Africans were free to choose their president in the first national elections open to all races, "Nkosi Sikelel' iAfrika" became the country's national anthem. It shares the stage with the former anthem of South Africans under Afrikaner rule, "Die Stem van Suid-Afrika" ("The Call of South Africa").

Zulu words

"Nkosi Sikelel' iAfrika"	Lord bless Africa
Maluphakamis's phondo lwayo	May her horn be raised
Yizwe imithandazo yethu	So also hear our prayers
Nkozi sikelele,	Lord bless us
Thina lusapho lwayo	We the families of Africa
Woza moya	Come spirit, bless us lord,
Woza moya	bless us
Woza moya oyingcwele	Come holy spirit
Nkosi sikekele	and bless our families
Thina lusapho lwayo	Lord take care of the nation
Sotho stanza	Stop the struggle
Morena boluka	and frustrations
Sechaba sahesu	Save it, save it
Ofedise dintoa lematsoenyeho	Save our nation,
Oseboloke Oseboloke	save it
Oseboloke morena oseboloke	
Sechaba sahesu	Our nation
Sechaba sa Afrika	Our Africa

brought covered wagons, and acted out the Great Trek. At night, the children formed wagon wheels while carrying oil lamps made from soft drink cans. Hooded riders staged a demonstration of their military tactics.

Terre'Blanche continued to threaten and terrorize black people who could not defend themselves. He was arrested and sentenced to six years in jail. One year was for beating up a black man and the other five years for the attempted murder of a black employee. By the time he was sentenced, the AWB movement had lost its power to threaten the new government.

Truth Commission

In 1995, Archbishop Tutu was chosen to head the Truth and Reconciliation Commission with Alex Boraine as his co-chairman. South Africa's former white rulers, the police, and the army had committed many acts of terrorism. They had tortured and murdered people. They had been responsible for depriving people of the most basic human rights. Families were destroyed.

The South African government created the Truth and Reconciliation Commission to find a way to bring these former enemies together. People who wanted to confess to crimes they had committed could appear before the committee and face the members of the family involved. The Commission members could decide whether to offer amnesty to those who had committed the crimes.

Winnie Mandikizela-Mandela arrives at TRC hearings in Johannesburg, surrounded by supporters as well as those accusing her of murder and other crimes.

Amnesty means forgiving someone for a crime he or she has committed. The families would finally know what had really happened. The commission had two years to conduct these hearings. Archbishop Tutu and Alex Boraine traveled all over the country, holding hearings. There was an outpouring of confessions and of grief.

In January 1997, five white police officers appeared before the Commission and admitted that they were the ones who murdered Steve Biko in 1977. In November 1997, Nelson Mandela's former wife, Winnie Mandikizela-Mandela, had to face charges she murdered a teenager and was responsible for the death of six others.

The Powerhouse of the African Continent

South Africa is the economic powerhouse of the African continent. Though it occupies just 4 percent of the land, and has only 6 percent of the population, it creates 25 percent of the continent's wealth and has 40 percent of the industrial production of the entire continent.

Some homes are shacks without plumbing.

THESE FIGURES CONCEAL AS MUCH ABOUT South Africa as they reveal. Most whites in South Africa (and a small number of blacks) live in comfortable homes, with clean water and electricity, and have automobiles. Many homes have swimming pools. They have jobs that pay well and allow them time to enjoy leisure activities. Their children attend schools that have computers, well-furnished classrooms, and enough textbooks for every student.

Townships and Poverty

But the vast majority of black South Africans live in a state of poverty, without electricity, clean water, or sanitation. Most of their homes are built by hand, out of any materials they can find. In the rural regions, houses may be built of mud and thatch, with wooden poles for support. In the urban townships, houses were built without running water or flush toilets. These were meant to be temporary homes, to be used only while a black person was working in a "white" city. For the millions who have lived in these townships, they are the only homes they have ever known. Now, they are slowly being upgraded but the job is enormous, and very expensive.

Opposite: **Platinum, more valuable than gold, is mined and refined at Rustenburg.**

Mandela Village, former squatter community, was helped by wealthier neighbors in Hout Bay.

South Africa's constitution guarantees its citizens decent housing. The problem is fulfilling that guarantee. Millions of people live in shacks that are barely one step away from being homeless. A flood of people looking for jobs is overwhelming the cities, especially Johannesburg and Cape Town. A typical shack is made of corrugated metal sheets called zincs, and then covered on the insides with paper and cardboard. People take discarded metal advertising signs and use them for part of a wall or a ceiling. In regions of the Cape, the shacks stretch out as far as the eye can see. Some of the communities are more than twenty years old now. Unable to stop the flow of people, the government has made these communities legitimate by paving the streets and providing water taps.

In one instance, a wealthy white community in Hout Bay, near Cape Town, woke up one morning to find a black squatter camp had sprung up just across the valley. Whites and blacks formed a working committee and agreed to limit the size of the camp in exchange for a supply of electricity and plumbing. The camp is called Mandela Village.

In most cases, however, bridging the gap between these two extremes is the government's most difficult task. Although South Africa is strong, economically, it will take years, perhaps even generations, to create a better standard of living for the millions of people who now live in these shacks.

Economy Built on Minerals

Immigrants coming to developed nations often say the "streets are paved with gold." In Johannesburg, this is nearly true. The city was built on the site of the gold lying beneath the surface. In addition to gold, South Africa has platinum reserves as well as diamonds. The Northern Province even calls itself "the Platinum Province" because the platinum mines are located there. South Africa is the world's biggest supplier of platinum. In addition to jewelry, platinum is a vital part of pollution control devices used in automobiles. Mining these minerals creates wealth for the companies that own the minerals. It also creates wealth for the government through taxes. The mines provide jobs for several hundred thousand workers.

South Africa still has huge mineral reserves that will provide employment for decades. It has about 40 percent of all the gold reserves in the world, more than three-quarters of all the platinum reserves and nearly three-quarters of all the chromium reserves. Its diamond reserves are much smaller but the De Beers companies control the marketing of about 80 percent of all the diamonds mined in the world.

The Mines

In the beginning, both the gold and diamond mines were worked as open-pit mines. When they became too deep to be mined in this way, the mines had to be worked from beneath the surface, as underground operations. Shafts and tunnels had to be built and this changed the entire nature of mining. When the work was near the surface, anyone with a pick and shovel and some money could buy a license and stake a claim.

Underground mining requires machinery and money and the South African mines were organized by a handful of big mining companies called houses.

The mines need huge numbers of workers to bring out the ore. They employ hundreds of thousands of miners, nearly all of them blacks. As the mines grew in this way, blacks did the hard labor in the mines. The managers and supervisors were white.

But when you go underground, no matter what your color, the work is very tough. Miners work in hot, humid, and dangerous tunnels. They don't see the sky or breathe fresh air all day long.

Most of the black Africans come to the mines to earn money and then go back to their homes, often hundreds of miles away. These migrant workers often don't see their families for six months or more at a time. Migratory labor became the pattern of life for hundreds of thousands of Africans.

There are many hazards for those seeking the steady employment that mining offers. Mining accidents claim lives every year. On average, one miner is killed for every ton of gold produced. Sometimes there are cave-ins at the mining site itself. Some of the worst accidents occur when a mine elevator fails. These huge, open elevators that take the miners down into the earth to the mining site can hold up to one hundred men. Most of these elevators and mine shafts are very old.

Although mining gold has been a great money-making operation, the mining firms have no control over the world gold price, which is set by five banks in England. Sometimes, the price drops down to a point where some of the old, very deep mines are no longer profitable to work. That means that it actually costs more, per ounce, to mine the gold, than the price people will pay for it. This happened in December 1977, when the price of gold dropped to $284 an ounce, the lowest price in twelve years.

Some South Africans work in the service industry.

Diversifying Industry

South Africa must concentrate on creating jobs that don't depend on minerals. These include manufacturing and service businesses. While there are millions of blacks who would like jobs, very few of them have been educated or trained for the business world. The old system of education had very limited goals for most blacks. Now, employees are being asked to favor black applicants who are seeking jobs. Often, blacks are employed even though they really can't do the job. This is called "window dressing" because it makes the company look good. Some blacks in South Africa are paid very good salaries for work they don't know how to do. Whites are being asked to work alongside these new black employees and teach them

What South Africa Grows, Makes, and Mines

Agriculture *(in U.S.dollars)*

Poultry and eggs	847,200,000
Beef cattle	571,200,000
Corn	307,400,000

Manufacturing *(in U.S.dollars)*

Chemicals	1,633,400,000
Processed foods and beverages	1,627,600,000
Iron and steel	1,331,600,000

Mining *(in U.S.dollars)*

Gold	4,589,000,000
Diamonds	3,099,000,000
Coal	1,912,600,000

their jobs. Whites are expected to train their own replacements. Many feel discouraged about their future in South Africa and are leaving the country. But it will take many years for blacks to make up for the education and experience they were once denied.

Today, however, South Africa's statistics paint a very gloomy picture. In 1991, out of nearly 18,000 engineers, only 30 were blacks. Of more than 2,000 pharmacists, only 31 were blacks.

Telkom is one firm that has worked hard to create jobs for blacks. Telkom is South Africa's telephone company. In 1993, at the tail end of the apartheid era, the company had 1 black employee out of 58,000 people. Within two years, it had hired nearly one hundred black managers. While the government doesn't set quotas on hiring blacks, it only awards contracts to companies that can show they have made progress in adding blacks to their workforce.

Tourism

One of the brightest areas of new employment is in the tourist industry. South Africa has a wealth of tourist attractions in addition to the wildlife parks. Tourist facilities include hotels, restaurants, and airlines as well as resorts and casinos. Cultural tourism is one of the newest trends in South Africa. Cultural "villages" offer a chance to experience traditional African life. Shakaland, in KwaZulu-Natal, was created from the location for the television series *Shaka Zulu*. Here, visitors can stay overnight and watch Zulu dances, eat authentic foods, and learn about Zulu fighting techniques and weapons.

The Valley of Waves resort in Sun City

Workers harvesting grapes at a winery

Sun City is the perfect symbol of both the old and the new South Africa. It was built by entrepreneur Sol Kerzner in the old homeland of Bophuthatswana. It took advantage of the "independent" status of Bop, as it is called. Sun City offered gambling at a time when it was not allowed in South Africa. Foreign entertainers who appeared there, at huge salaries, were condemned for supporting apartheid.

Agriculture

Agriculture brought the first white people to South Africa. When the Dutch first arrived, they planted food crops including grapes for wine. Within three years of Jan van Riebeeck's landing, he had planted vines imported from Europe and South Africa's wine industry began. In 1659, the first wine was made from grapes grown at the Cape.

Today, its wines enjoy an excellent reputation and the country is the ninth-largest wine producer in the world. Local residents complain that they can't find their favorite wines anymore because so much of the wine is exported. Exports of wines jumped 600 percent in just six years.

The vineyards are located near Cape Town where the growing conditions are favorable. Traditionally, most of the workers were Coloureds who lived in the region. Now blacks also work in the vineyards although the management is nearly all white.

Farming once occupied most South Africans. Today, farming accounts for only 4 percent of the country's economy but most people in the rural areas still grow food for their own use. Even when rainfall is good, farming accounts for less than 5 percent of the country's overall economic production. The single most important crop is maize (corn), used for flour. The country needs more than

South African Currency

The South African unit of currency is called the rand, named after the ridge of land where the gold mines are situated. A rand is worth about twenty cents in American money (as of December 1997). One rand is divided into one hundred cents.

Each bill is a different size depending on its value. The smallest bill is worth ten rands, the largest is two hundred rands. Each is also a different color, making it quite easy to tell the bills apart, even for people who cannot read. The currency is made with a metallic thread running through it to prevent counterfeiting. It costs about R1.50, that is, one-and a-half-rands, to ride to work on a bus.

All of the bills feature the country's wildlife along with another important part of the economy. The fifty-rand note, which is pink, features a male lion. On the reverse is an illustration of SASOL, a chemical plant that processes coal into gasoline. SASOL was created during apartheid because South Africa feared it might not be able to get the oil it needed.

A prosperous farm in Kwa-Zulu-Natal, where ostriches are allowed to roam free.

Sugarcane grows well in the hot and humid climate of KwaZulu-Natal.

six million tons a year and only produces that much in a very good year. In years with little rainfall, it must import maize from other countries.

Farming is difficult in South Africa because it is a low rain-fall area. Its large-scale farmers, most of them Afrikaners, have the ability to grow enormous amounts of food under better farming conditions. The governments of South Africa and Mozambique signed an agreement allowing a group of farmers to settle in neighboring Mozambique's northern province of

Niassa. Their leader is Constand Viljoen, who was the most famous general in the South African army, under the old government. Other farmers have established farms in other countries including Zambia. Their farms are very successful there because the land and climate are so good.

Investment in tourist facilities is considered a key to South Africa's economic future. In the region around the St. Lucia Wetlands, considered one of the most important natural resources of the country, a plan to develop a mine was stopped by environmental activists. Now, the government hopes the St. Lucia Wetlands Park will become one of the biggest tourist attractions in the country. They are hoping for massive investment in the region which would create about two thousand long-term jobs.

Cyril Ramaphosa

Cyril Ramaphosa, a Zulu-speaking lawyer, came to the public eye in 1984 as leader of the National Union of Mineworkers (NUM). Ramaphosa's skill as a negotiator, working to earn pay raises and better working conditions for the miners, opened the eyes of many whites in government. His skills as a negotiator made them question their long-held beliefs that blacks had limited intelligence. As a result, he was named to lead the committee to write the country's new constitution. When the constitution was completed, he moved into the economic area. He now directs Johnnies Industrial Corp., nicknamed Johnnic. Forty percent of the shares are held by black economic groups.

Phone service, including cellular phones, is readily available and dependable in the white areas and in the wealthier black

areas. At the same time, many of the country's people are without any phone service. Although telephone service is generally restricted to urban areas and white farms, South Africa is far ahead of other African countries. Now, South Africa's telephone companies are moving into those other countries to modernize their systems. In some cases, where telephone service is very limited, they are moving ahead to the most modern, fiber optic systems or even just installing cellular systems and not using land lines at all. This cuts down on the possibility of vandalism and is much less expensive to set up. In 1997, the cell phone industry signed up its millionth customer.

The black middle class often uses cellular phones, while some people have no phone service at all.

Although many South Africans lack electricity and indoor plumbing, many others are busy working at their computers and joining the world online. Internet cafes may be found in the big cities and web addresses are routinely included in news stories.

South Africa needs tremendous amounts of money to build factories and create hundreds of thousands of new jobs. Business people and newly elected officials lost no time in traveling to the United States and other foreign countries, trying to interest companies in investing in South Africa.

International Investments Return

The investments began in 1991, when sanctions against South Africa ended. Within a few years, the amount of money invested by U.S. companies came to more than one billion dollars. Half of that came from manufacturing companies ranging from the Ford Motor Company to Levi Straus blue jeans. More than 350 U.S. companies are now directly involved, or have investments, in South Africa. The Levi's factory in Epping, the industrial area near Cape Town, employs 230 workers, most of them women.

U.S. companies are investing in South Africa.

One of the surest signs of South Africa's economic recovery was the appearance of McDonald's fast food restaurants. They didn't come without a fight, however. A South African who owned a local chain of fast food stores tried to use the trademark himself. McDonald's had to go to the Supreme Court in Johannesburg to defend its right to its own trademark. When

A McDonald's restaurant in Cape Town

McDonald's won, many U.S. company executives were relieved. They felt that South Africa was finally a secure place in which to invest. When the first McDonald's opened in South Africa, it made front page news in the local newspapers. On opening day, twenty thousand people were served at one of the new restaurants in Johannesburg.

The Hard Rock Café had to face another problem. Two clubs using that name already existed in South Africa.

Crime in South Africa

The security industry is one of the fastest-growing parts of the economy. Its success is a response to the other fastest growing business—crime. The lack of jobs has driven many people to lives of crime. Crowded together in the cities, many feel they have no other choice. Many are also angry. There are many young men, men in their twenties, who sacrificed their education in order to disrupt life in the townships. This was the only way they knew to force a change in the government. When that change finally came, they found that their lack of education made them unfit for employment. In their despair, many have turned to crime.

Most of the crimes they commit are against their neighbors, who are often just as poor as they are. Hillbrow, a section of Johannesburg, was once known for its coffee shops and bookstores. It became the first place black people moved to after the "influx" laws changed. These were the laws that kept black people from living in the cities. But too many people came at once. They crowded into the apartments and often could not find employment. Rents were not paid, drug dealing began, and the crime rate soared.

Some criminals work for crime bosses. They concentrate on more profitable crimes against wealthy people, black and white. Carjacking has become one of the most feared crimes in these areas. Many drivers have been killed during carjackings, and it has made driving one of the most fearful activities. The value of the property stolen is bigger than all but a few industries in South Africa.

The increase in crime occurred just as the South African police force was trying to deal with the dramatic changes in the country. Under apartheid, the police

Crime prevention unit makes an arrest in Hillbrow, the black entertainment section of Johannesburg.

spent their time enforcing apartheid laws, not fighting crime. When apartheid ended, they were not prepared to fight real crime. The time it took them to change their methods gave the criminals virtually a free ride. Crime soared: the murder rate in South Africa was the highest in the world, more than nine times that of the United States. Many people left because the country had become too dangerous to live in. It took more than two years before the police began to get violent crime under control.

Local people didn't know they weren't the real thing since they used the Hard Rock's familiar sign and name. Rather than go to court, the management bought out the fake clubs and closed them down. And then they opened a 400-seat Hard Rock Café at the Victoria and Alfred Waterfront in Cape Town.

South African Breweries is one of the biggest employers in the country, with a workforce of one hundred thousand people. The beer is consumed locally and also exported to neighboring countries.

Those who find employment in firms such as these are in the minority. An estimated two million people earn some kind of living in the "informal sector." This includes women who make crafts or bake breads, as well as people who sit on the sidewalks and under trees selling a tiny stock of gum or candies. Some have small shops, called spaza shops, in the black communities. They sell a variety of items including groceries. Under apartheid, these were often the only places where residents of townships could shop without traveling to white-owned stores in the cities. The combined sale of all these small shops and street vendors amounts to about 7 percent of the nation's economic output.

Sidewalk vendors sit outside, in hot weather and in the rain, waiting for customers. These hawkers, as they are called, reflect one of the most visible changes in South African cities. There was a time, in the small, most conservative towns, when black people were expected to step off the sidewalk into the street to allow a white person to pass by. Now, the sidewalks in some parts of the cities more closely resemble those in other parts of Africa.

A lively crafts market can be found outside the main train station in Cape Town. It's also the site of the central tourist office. It's an ideal place for the vendors because a steady stream of tourists passes by every day. In Durban, female street vendors have formed their own union, the Self-Employed Women's Union, to protect their rights. The cities now truly reflect the population of South Africa.

Street vendors sell to the tourists of Durban.

South African Armed Forces

The role of the South African Defense Forces changed completely with the end of white rule. At one time the army was engaged in wars in Namibia and Angola. It tried to stop those countries from becoming independent. They gained their independence anyway. The South African Defense Forces then took part in civil wars in those countries. When South Africa became a democratic country, all of these illegal actions stopped. The country no longer needed such a big army and many soldiers were discharged.

Ships of the South African Navy, including the S.A.S. *Drakensberg*, spend some of their time on goodwill missions around the world. Its men and women often are called upon to help transport goods during emergencies. They even play a role in Antarctica; South Africa is one of twelve members of the Scientific Committee on Antarctic Research. That icy continent is located due south of South Africa.

The Port of Durban

South Africa's major port city, Durban, on the Indian Ocean, serves much of southern Africa. Its modern facilities are well maintained. It is a reliable port where shippers know their goods will not sit out on the docks until they spoil in the sun. That is often what happens in ports in other countries along the same coast. Durban is South Africa's main cargo port. Rail lines carry goods from the port all over southern Africa.

The "Maputo Corridor," a land route that links the port of Maputo in Mozambique to the Gauteng area of South Africa, provides an alternative to the port at Durban. It is a very successful example of the cooperation now possible since South Africa became a democratic country and since peace has come to Mozambique.

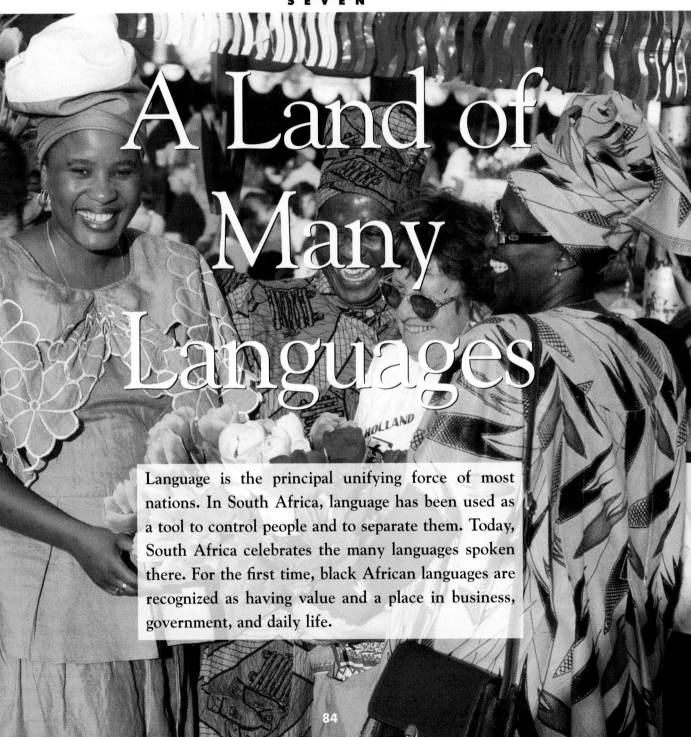

A Land of Many Languages

Language is the principal unifying force of most nations. In South Africa, language has been used as a tool to control people and to separate them. Today, South Africa celebrates the many languages spoken there. For the first time, black African languages are recognized as having value and a place in business, government, and daily life.

This Cape Malay girl is descended from the Malays brought to South Africa as forced labor.

ACCORDING TO THE CONSTITUTION, the official languages of South Africa are: Sepedi, Sesotho, Setswana, siSwati, Tshivenda, Xitsonga, Afrikaans, English, isiNdebele, isiXhosa and isiZulu. English, the language of business, is the only official language that is used internationally. Afrikaans is spoken throughout the country by Afrikaners, Coloureds, and many people who learned it in school.

Both the national government and the provincial government must use at least two of the official languages in official business. Citizens in any area of the country can expect to deal with the government by speaking their own language.

The constitution also recognizes the languages spoken by the Khoi, Nama, and San (the first inhabitants of South Africa), as well as sign language.

Each of the "black" languages is spoken by a distinct group of Africans. For example, IsiZulu is spoken by the Zulu people who dominate the province of KwaZulu Natal, but it is also spoken by Zulus wherever they live. While the homelands no longer exist as separate states, people continue to live in those regions.

Opposite: **Xhosa-speaking women dressed in traditional clothes were organizers of a charity carnival in Wynberg, Cape Town.**

There is a large Xhosa population in Crossroads.

Transkei and Ciskei are the former homelands of the Xhosa people. The Xhosas are the second largest ethnic group in South Africa. They number about seven million. IsiXhosa is the first language of President Mandela. It is known to westerners as the "click" language because it includes "pops," or clicks, when it is spoken. The "X" stands for a click sound. In the Roman alphabet, there is no letter to express the sound of that click.

Many Xhosas and Zulus migrated to the cities looking for work. A large Xhosa population lives in Crossroads and other settlements in the Cape Flats near Cape Town. They have increased the population of the region by about two million. They travel back to Transkei using the Transkei Express, a bus service created by enterprising Xhosas who recognized the need. Zulus are concentrated in Soweto, South Africa's biggest black township. But Xhosas, Tswanas, and people of other language groups also live there. As they mix, these people tend to learn each other's language. Most people in

Soweto speak several languages. Zulu, Xhosa, Tswana, and Ndebele people speak languages that are part of the same language group. They are known as the Nguni-speaking people. In Soweto, the casual mixing of languages, especially among young people, has led to a special township dialect. In the province of Gauteng, which includes Soweto, five languages may be used in a single household.

The other major language group is Sotho-Tswana. This group includes languages spoken by the Pedi, Twsana, and Sotho people, who live in the northeastern part of the country. Tswana-speaking people make up the population of the neighboring country of Botswana. Sotho-speaking people live in the country of Lesotho. These populations were sep-

An Afrikaner farmer

The Official Languages of South Africa

Afrikaans	Sesotho
English	Setswana
isiNdebele	siSwati
isiXhosa	Tshivenda
isiZulu	Xitsonga
Sepedi	

arated politically when the countries' were drawn up by Europeans.

SiSwati is spoken by the Swazi people who live in the province of Mpumalanga. It is the same language spoken by the people of Swaziland.

Languages do not stay the same. Change may come from new technology or words may be adopted because they describe an activity so well. The Afrikaans word *trek*, for example, has become part of everyday English.

Many educated adults in the Coloured community speak both English and Afrikaans and can easily switch back and forth. In meetings, speakers often alternate between two languages. In

Gustav Preller

Afrikaners have always felt the need to protect and nurture their language. In 1905, when Gustav Preller, a newspaper editor, published his first article on the subject, Afrikaans was considered the language of poor, uneducated whites. Many words in common use were borrowed from regional languages: Xhosa, English, and Malay, in addition to Dutch. The wealthier, better-educated whites spoke Dutch. Mr. Preller urged people to use more Dutch words in place of those Coloured words. He started a magazine written in this "purified" Afrikaans. His campaign was remarkably successful. In 1925, Afrikaans was named an official language of the Union of South Africa, replacing Dutch. (The only other official language was English.)

films and plays produced for the local audience, it's common to have the actors speak more than one language. South Africa is truly a multilingual nation.

Television, once owned and controlled by the government, has made the most dramatic shift in the use of language since 1990. Once there were two channels, one for English and one for Afrikaans. Now, the news may be in Zulu or Xhosa, English or Afrikaans. On some news programs, interviewers may speak one language while the person being interviewed answers in another language.

In the Cape, the constant mixing of English and Afrikaans has resulted in a dialect called *kombuis Afrikaans*, which means "kitchen Afrikaans."

Television incorporates some of the many languages of South Africa.

Spiritual Lives

Religious beliefs are at the heart of South Africa's existence as a nation. The French Huguenots were seeking religious freedom when they fled their European homes and made the dangerous journey to Africa. A belief in a strict Calvinist form of Christianity led the Afrikaners to their narrow interpretation of the Bible and ultimately to the policy of apartheid. During the time of the Great Trek, many Afrikaners believed the Bible was the only book they needed to guide them in their lives. Ultimately, this led to the idea of apartheid.

THE ZION CHRISTIAN CHURCH IS THE FASTEST GROWING religious movement in South Africa. Founded in 1910 by Engenas Lekganyane, the church counts a membership of more than five million black South Africans. They wear silver stars pinned onto a piece of green and black cloth. They take their name, Zion, from the Mount of Zion in Jerusalem. The church is a movement with a strong Christian core, adjusted to suit the way these Africans choose to worship. For example, they permit polygamy, the practice of having more than one wife at a time. They do not permit smoking, drinking alcohol, or eating pork. They feel very close connections to their ancestors, as do most traditional African peoples.

Although some Zionists accept Western medicine, they put most of their trust in faith healing, the belief that faith is the strongest medicine of all. They are vigorously opposed to sangomas, the traditional healers who play an important role in African life.

The Religions of South Africa	
Black independent churches	19%
Dutch Reformed	11%
Roman Catholic	8%
Methodist	7%
Anglican	5%
Lutheran	3%
Other Christian churches	25%
Indigenous religions	11%
Other	11%

Opposite:
Traditional healers

Sangomas are called to their profession, often in a dream. In Zulu areas, the sangoma is a well-respected figure. Many sangomas are women, and they are easily identified by their distinctive headdress. Beads often fall in front of a sangoma's face, partially blocking a clear view of her face. The sangoma tells of events that will affect an individual's life in the future.

Approximately 200,000 traditional healers practice in South Africa.

Spiritual and physical well-being are closely connected in African life. People ask their traditional healers for medicines to cure their problems as well as their illnesses. About two hundred thousand traditional healers practice in South Africa. This includes those who have a wide knowledge of natural substances such as herbs, tree roots, and other plants. Some healers have the knowledge of dozens of plants. The plants they prescribe are now being assessed by commercial drug companies. Healers are different from witch doctors, who use superstition to influence the people who consult them. Traditional healers know their patients well because they live in the same community. They take the patient's entire history into consideration and can be quite skilled in pinpointing a person's disease or illness.

The separation of church and state, the belief that government should not be involved with religion, is a new idea in South Africa. Under the white government, the Dutch Reformed Church was synonymous with the National Party. The Dutch Reformed Church and the laws governing the nation were in complete harmony. The Dutch Reformed Church arrived in South Africa in 1652 with the first Dutch settlers. It narrowly follows the ideas of John Calvin and offers its members

Archbishop Desmond Tutu

In South Africa during apartheid, one church leader stood out for his willingness to speak out. Anglican Archbishop Desmond Mpilo Tutu turned his pulpit into a platform opposing apartheid.

As a moral and spiritual leader, he questioned the morals of other Christians, the leaders of the National Party. When the government wrote a new constitution in 1983, which gave limited rights to Coloureds and Asians but not to blacks, Tutu spoke out against it. In 1986, he became very political in his opposition to apartheid by supporting economic sanctions against South Africa. In that year, he was named Anglican Archbishop despite the fact that blacks and white members of the Anglican Church could not attend the same services. He also put himself into mortal danger by saving a man from the fury of a crowd in a black township. In 1984, he was awarded the Nobel Prize for Peace.

Baptism is an important part of the Zion Baptist Church. More than 5 million black South Africans follow this religion.

a very strict path. There is no singing or joyfulness in this solemn church whose buildings are without ornamentation.

It was this church that fervently believed in the policy of apartheid. In 1960 the World Council of Churches condemned the Dutch Reformed Church for this policy. The church refused to change, and it was barred from the Council. Many whites felt ashamed of the way their church treated blacks but were afraid to go against the church since that also meant defying the government. One who spoke out was Reverend Beyers Naudé. He suffered greatly for his beliefs. For seven years he was banned and sometimes also placed under house arrest.

In addition to whites, about three-quarters of a million Coloureds belong to the Dutch Reformed Church. Most speak Afrikaans as their first language, giving them strong ties to the

Afrikaner community. Of course they opposed apartheid, declaring that it was a sin. Their principal leader was the Reverend Allan Boesak, a Coloured, who was a key player in the National Council of Churches' decision to eject the Dutch Reformed Church. Rev. Boesak, who was married to a Coloured

Reverend Allan Boesak

woman and had four children, lost his position as a religious leader when he became involved with a white woman. The Coloured community was furious with him. He had betrayed his own religious beliefs. He lost his leadership role and eventually left South Africa entirely. Later he was accused of taking funds meant for community use. He was brought back to South Africa to stand trial.

The end of apartheid stunned many devout Afrikaners. They had lived their lives according to the teachings of their church. It had been the core element of their lives, and they had to admit that those teachings were wrong, and many have been left in despair. Others insisted that apartheid was right and broke away from the main Dutch Reformed Church. The conservative churches they follow offer the kind of moral support they need.

The Grey Street Mosque

Other Religions

Other religions also play important roles in everyday life in South Africa. The Malay community, descended from slaves that were brought to South Africa more than three hundred years ago, are devout Muslims. Although the Dutch did not allow them to practice their religion, they managed to keep their beliefs alive through the centuries. The first Muslim mosque was built in 1798, in Cape Town. Recently, the Malay community celebrated the three-hundredth-anniversary of the Koran, the Muslim holy book, in South Africa.

A Muslim rally against drugs

Their members do not drink alcohol or eat pork. During apartheid, most of the Malay community was moved from their homes on the slopes of Table Mountain in Cape Town to the Cape Flats. A small group managed to stay on in a section called Bo-Kaap.

These crowded communities, where unemployment was high, became breeding grounds for gangs and drugs. The religious Muslims lived in fear and felt the police were not able, or willing, to stop the gangs. They formed their own group, PAGAD (People Against Gangsterism and Drugs). They

Opposite: **A Hindu shop catering to the Asians who reside in Durban**

often hold rallies in Cape Town to draw attention to their demands for more protection. But some have gone much farther and have formed vigilante groups. In a way, they have become as lawless as the people they set out to remove from their community.

The Asians who were brought to South Africa in the 1860s as laborers on the sugarcane plantations in Natal also brought their own religions with them. Most are Hindus but there is also a community of Asian Muslims. Hindu temples and Muslim mosques were built to meet the needs of the growing community. In Durban, center of the Asian community in South Africa, both Hindu and Moslem holy buildings are found. People from the two religions rarely marry though they share a common ethnic heritage.

The Jewish Community

The first Jewish synagogue was built in Cape Town, in 1863. Most of the Jews are descended from Lithuanians who fled religious persecution in Europe. The earliest arrivals lived in District Six where the last Jewish bookstore still stands amid the rubble. The community grew to about 120,000 and then remained at that number as people began to leave South Africa during the apartheid years. Jews have had a strong influence on South Africa's economic and cultural life. When crime increased in white areas in the 1990s, many Jews left the country. The Jewish community is now believed to number fewer than one hundred thousand. Most live in the suburbs of Johannesburg and Cape Town.

Leisure Life

From the foot-stomping gumboot dance of the Zulus to the symphony orchestra and ballet of the cities, South Africa's many cultures enjoy a very wide variety of music, dance, art, and theater. Because of the enormous number of languages used in the country, most of the cultural activities are enjoyed by specific language groups.

Actors depicting the lives of slaves in a musical titled *Klop Klop*

THERE ARE A FEW EVENTS that unite the entire country: sporting events. South Africa is a nation that is sports mad. During apartheid, the country was banned from most international sports competitions. It was expelled from Olympic competition in 1970, but had not competed since 1960 because so many other nations had threatened to boycott the Games if South Africa was allowed to compete. This denied young people their chance to compete against the best in the world. It made the athletes wonder if they were the best, or just the best in South Africa.

Some gave up their citizenship and moved to other countries to be able to compete while they were in their prime. Sydney Maree, a brilliant miler, became a U.S. citizen and competed for the United States during his running career. He returned to South Africa in the 1990s to head a sporting company. Many others could not afford to leave or were not willing to leave their homes and families.

Opposite: **Zulus take part in an annual dance championship in Durban.**

Sydney Maree running in
the New York Mile

South Africa performed
well in the 1996 Olympic
Games. Among the athletes
were men's marathon
runner Josia Thugwane.

In 1991, the Olympic com-
mittee readmitted South
Africa to the competition. It
was barely a year before the
1992 games in Barcelona,
not enough time to put
together a full, multiracial
team. Still, 120 South
African athletes and staff
went to the Games. Nearly
all were white, a legacy of
apartheid when blacks had
little access to sports training
and facilities. Runner Elana
Meyer brought home a silver
medal in the 10,000-meter
race. Then in 1996, South
Africa participated fully at
the Atlanta Centenary
Games in the United States.
The results were better than
expected: Josia Thugwane
won the gold medal in the
men's marathon, and swim-
mer Penny Heyns won two
gold medals.

Swimmer Penny Heyns won two gold medals in the 1996 Olympics.

Olympic runner Elana Meyer

Rugby is an important sport for many South Africans.

South Africa joyfully announced its return to international competition at the 1995 World Rugby Cup competition. The South African team had just one black player among the whites but that one proved to be the star. South Africa was the host and was proud to show off at its first international event. Against all odds, the South African Springboks won the World Cup, beating heavily favored New Zealand. After the victory, people danced in the streets, blacks and whites celebrating together. The motto for the event was "One Team, One Nation."

In spite of this success, rugby is a white sport in South Africa. Blacks all over Africa devote most of their sporting energy and interest to soccer. The soccer team soon proved it was equal to the task of uniting the nation. When South Africa also won the African Nations' Cup for the first team, the leading player was Mark Williams. This Coloured soccer player carried the team, and the nation, to victory. The nickname of the team, Bafana Bafana, was on the front page of newspaper across the country. It's taken from the Zulu word for "boys."

Professional soccer in South Africa

The Cape to Rio yacht race was held in South Africa in 1993, the first time since 1979. This treacherous race in the South Atlantic Ocean begins in Cape Town and ends in Rio de Janeiro, Brazil, and takes three to four weeks to complete. The race, held every three years, sets off from Cape Town's harbor with Table Mountain in the background.

The 1996 Cape to Rio yacht race

Willie Mtolo first came to the United States in 1992 to run in the famous marathon that winds through the streets of New York City. To the delight of South Africans, he won this event and was cheered all along the 26.2-mile (45-km) long route. The New York Road Runners Club was thrilled that Mtolo competed in his first international race in New York.

South Africans made a major effort to win the honor of hosting the 2004 Olympic Games. The host city of Cape

Willie Mtolo, the winner of the New York Marathon in 1992

Town would have been seen all over the world by anyone with a television set. The city had counted on the Games to bring in investment money. Money is needed to build houses, to improve roads, and to erect sports stadiums. These facilities would have been used by the local people after the Olympics. The Olympic bid logo, a beautiful swirl of the Olympic colors in the form of the African continent, was seen on everything from the front page of the local newspaper to lapel pins. The Games had never been held in Africa, and South Africans believed the time was right. They even painted a South

African Airways jumbo jet in the Olympic colors for the team that traveled to the Atlanta Games in 1996. When the short list of cities under consideration was announced in March 1997, Cape Town was included along with Athens, Buenos Aires, Rome, and Stockholm. Ultimately, Athens was named the host city for the 2004 games.

Rich Cultural Traditions

When the stage shifts from sports to music, South Africa's rich cultural traditions are on display. Plays have been used to tell stories of each community's triumphs and tragedies. One song-writer pair teamed up ten years ago in spite of the problems they faced. David Kramer is white; his partner, Taliep Petersen, is Malay. The subject they share is the story of District Six. Their plays, full of music and dance, are a mix of English and Afrikaans.

Writer Nadine Gordimer

As South Africa's people have struggled with apartheid, and life after apartheid, their stories have been told in novels by Nadine Gordimer. Her books were banned by the white government because she told those stories too honestly. When she wrote *July's People*, a novel that told about a future South

Zulu Culture

What does it mean to be a Zulu? That is a question musician Johnny Clegg has been asked throughout his career. Although Clegg is white, he is known for his Zulu songs and for dancing the thundering foot stomping dance of the Zulus. Clegg, along with Sipho Mchunu, his Zulu partner for many years, performed in spite of the restrictions. Clegg was a poor, uneducated white boy of sixteen when he became friendly with some Zulu musicians. Throughout the years, he studied and then taught anthropology. At the same time, he absorbed the Zulu music, language, and culture. He has spent his life performing Zulu music and dance. He and guitarist Sipho Mchunu formed a musical group called Juluka (which means sweat). Their act defied the idea of apartheid: a black gardener and a white university student were not supposed to share a culture.

Africa with blacks and whites engaged in a civil war, she was trying to help the whites think about the future. Because of the bans, her books were often better known outside South Africa. In 1991, Ms. Gordimer was awarded the Nobel Prize for Literature.

Choral singing, without musical accompaniment, brings out some of South Africa's best voices. Groups compete to win prizes, and recognition. The best known choral group from South Africa is Ladysmith Black Mambazo, led by Joseph Shabalala. Their sweet harmony is now so well recognized the

Ladysmith Black Mambazo with Paul Simon in Zimbawe before the end of apartheid

group was chosen to do the background singing for a television commercial. Named for the town of Ladysmith, in KwaZulu, the group caught the ear of singer/songwriter Paul Simon. Their voices and many Zulu phrases were part of *Graceland*, the album they recorded together.

Radio

For most South Africans who live in the rural areas, radio provides all their entertainment and information. Radio programs offer the widest variety of languages, tailored to each local area. News, weather, entertainment, and many kinds of educational programs fill the airwaves. Most of these people listen on battery-operated radios.

Radio 702, one of the most popular stations in South Africa, sponsored a crafts show. John and Gary, two of the station's talk show hosts, offered radios to people all over the Gauteng region and told them to decorate or design objects using

Coloureds' Carnival

Each year, on New Year's Day, hundreds of Coloured people take to the streets of Cape Town to celebrate the annual Coloureds' Carnival. Groups of minstrels paint their faces, wear matching costumes, and carry tiny, colorful umbrellas as they dance and sing their way through town.

The Coloureds' Carnival owes much of its look and sound to the sailors of the American Civil War. In the 1860s, the Confederate ship the *Alabama* found a friendly port in distant Cape Town. The local people quickly picked up the sailors' music and imitated it. Few of the people who take part in the Carnival know this bit of odd history but to a visiting American, the symbols are easy to read. The songs they sing are American, usually from 1940s and 1950s.

During the worst years of apartheid, the minstrels were not allowed to parade through the streets; they had to hold their celebration in a stadium. Since the end of apartheid they joyfully reclaim the streets on this one day and night.

the radios and any other materials they chose. The result was the Radio Show, an exhibit at the Everard Reade gallery in Rosebank, a suburb of Johannesburg. One person painted jazz scenes on wooden cases and another sculpted an African woman holding the radio. One made radio cases out of tins used for beer and shaped them like trucks. One Ndebele artist, Emmly Masanabo, combined traditional Ndebele beadwork and house painting for her radio.

Traveling circuses have long been popular in South Africa. Through all the years of apartheid, and continuing today, small circuses have brought excitement and wildlife to many of the smallest towns in the country. The Osler circus was a familiar sight in the 1970s and 1980s as Keith Anderson took his little troupe around the country. Anderson took many teenagers off the street and trained them in acrobatics, design, and the business of running a circus.

Robben Island

Robben Island, South Africa's newest museum, opened on January 1, 1997, and is already its most famous. The museum was once the prison home of Nelson Mandela who spent eighteen of his twenty-seven years in jail there. Both the tiny cell in which he was confined and the limestone quarry where he broke rocks are now part of a carefully regulated tourist site.

Although there were many ordinary criminals on Robben Island, it was the political prisoners, like Mandela, who made the prison famous. Located just 5 miles (8 km) off the coast from Cape Town, the prison island became known as the University of Robben Island. Younger black activists were jailed with older, better educated political prisoners. Through the years, after their hard labor for the day was complete, an informal school allowed one generation to pass along its knowledge and experience to the next.

Art and Artists

The South African National Gallery in Cape Town offers exhibits of African art and craft as well as works by European artists. It is located right in the Company Gardens, where Jan van Riebeeck began growing food for the men and families that came to Africa from Holland. On display are works by Willie Bester, South Africa's best-known artist. Museum Afrika in Johannesburg opened in 1994, on the site of an abandoned warehouse, next to the Market Theatre. Its first exhibition was a massive show of art from all over the world, the Johannesburg Biennale. The show included many local, unknown artists. Many of them came from the townships.

In District Six, a church has been turned into a museum that commemorates the community that was destroyed. Hanging from the ceiling are some of the old street signs: Hanover Street, Reform Street, Springfield Street, de Korte Street, Van de Leur Street. The man responsible for directing the destruction of the district could not bear to throw the signs away. He hid them in his basement for twenty years and then gave them to the museum. A map on the floor shows all the streets. The residents are now coming back to write their names on the map and show where their families used to live.

A Day in the Life of South Africa

There are as many typical ways of living in South Africa as there are different languages and cultures. Each culture has its own foods, rituals, costume, music. In the rural areas, life is ruled by chiefs. The chief decides how much land a family has and settles disputes. The chief is the law for the people who live in the region.

W
ITHIN MOST CULTURES there are poor people and rich people. Farmers live different lives than city people. Some people live in small houses made of thatch and mud while others build houses of wood or brick. Some people live in apartments in the city, others live in small houses in the suburbs and in the countryside.

Weather does not play a great role in the way people live in South Africa. Winters are mild, and a person can live an entire lifetime in most of the country without ever seeing snow. The major exception is on the higher elevations of mountains such as the Drakensbergs.

Money plays an enormous role in determining the quality of a person's life. And race still plays an equally important role because most South Africans continue to lead the same kind of life they lived before apartheid ended. While many black South Africans have better jobs, better homes, and better foods to eat, most are still living very much as they always have.

Typical old Cape Dutch architecture

Opposite: **Zulu beehive huts**

Mealie Paps and Boerewors

The foods white and black people eat represent their different cultures. White people are used to choosing from a wide variety of foods, having something different for each of their meals, day after day.

Poor black people usually have a porridge made from maize flour called mealie pap. Maize is a kind of corn. This dish is eaten every day by many black South Africans. In the cities, black women can buy maize flour that is already prepared. In the rural areas, they will grow their own maize and then pound it into a flour before it can be cooked. Ears of corn are also called mealies. Roasted mealies are a favorite food.

Afrikaners enjoy barbecues just as Americans do (above). They call them braais. The pleasant climate makes it possible to cook outdoors most of the year. A typical braai always includes boerewors, a sausage made with a variety of meats. The spices that are used are often a family recipe. Afrikaners take great pride in their homemade boerewors. Another Afrikaner dish is bobotie, a kind of stew made with meat.

Another typical South African food is biltong. Made of meat that has been dried, biltong is similar to meat jerky, but much more delicious. It can be made of any kind of meat and in South Africa that may be ostrich meat.

There is a relationship in South Africa that did not end when apartheid was written off the law books. This is the relationship between a white woman and her black maid.

The gap in their lifestyles is played out every single day. The maid travels from a black township, using buses, trains, or taxis. These aren't the kinds of cars we call taxis. They are minivans meant to hold nine to twelve people. Instead, most of them are packed with up to twenty people. Some have to stand in the aisle and stoop over all the way. It often takes a black person two or three such rides to arrive at the home of their employer in the suburbs. The maid may not have electricity or hot water at home.

When she arrives at work, she passes through the locked gate. A wall surrounds the property that always has a lovely garden, a place for children to play, and often, a swimming pool. There are expensive cars in the driveway. The house has all the latest kitchen equipment and several bathrooms fitted out with excellent plumbing.

Teenage South Africans

Teenagers' lives are just as different as the lives of their parents. The rituals they go through depend very much on where they live. For boys in their teens, daily life is a routine established by the parents. In the city, teens go to Raves, dance parties that go on all night. They are very expensive for South Africa, costing as much as thirty rand (about $7) admission. That's twice as much as it costs to go to a movie. Teens are attracted by the mystery that surrounds the Raves. They are

Wire Toys

Children like to play with wire toys that are made at home. Many people have become very skilled at taking bits of wire and twisting them into objects with wheels. The toy may be in the shape of a bicycle, or it may show a man on a wheel. The wire extends into a handle that the child uses to push the toy along the ground.

When visitors began buying these wire toys, the people who make them were encouraged to create more complicated pieces. Wire motorcycles, wire saxophones, and whole wire orchestras are now offered by street vendors.

always held in different sites such as an old movie studio on the edge of Soweto or an unused warehouse on a distant pier at the Cape Town harbor. The harder they are to get to, the more people they seem to attract.

Coloured teenagers socialize with their own race group

In the rural areas, a ceremonial party for teenagers is more likely to be held when boys enter a new stage of life. This is usually at the time of circumcision, which takes place during the teen years. A feast is prepared and the ceremony takes place with the whole community involved. Boys go away from their families. They spend time with the elders, who teach them about their history and culture. Once a boy has gone through this ceremony, he is considered an adult member of his community.

Health Care

The quality and availability of health care in South Africa varies enormously. In the cities, there is about one doctor for every 700 people but in the most isolated rural areas, that jumps to about 10,000 to 30,000. In reality it means that most

people do not have access to health care. South Africa and the United States are the only two industrial countries that do not offer their people a national health plan.

South Africa has an enormous AIDS infection rate. It is estimated that one and a half million people have been infected with the HIV virus that causes AIDS. In addition, a tuberculosis epidemic has made this disease one of the worst in the country. Every year, ten thousand South Africans die from TB, which is a curable disease.

South Africa is well known as the place where the world's first heart transplant was performed. Dr. Christiaan Barnard performed the surgery at Groote Schuur Hospital in Cape Town in 1967.

President Mandela's private life has been a victim of his political career. Both of his marriages ended in divorce. His first wife, Evelyn, was left alone while he was working to end apartheid. He was in jail for twenty-seven of the thirty-eight years he was married to his second wife, Winnie. When he was released from prison, he found they really had no marriage. She had suffered greatly during his years in prison and became a cruel and violent person. He was embarrassed by her behavior and the criminal charges brought against her, and they were divorced in 1995. Now, his companion is Graca Machel, widow of Samora Machel, who led his nation, Mozambique, to independence. Graca Machel and Nelson Mandela are veterans of Africa's fight for independence.

Soon after Nelson Mandela was elected president, he announced he would serve only one five-year term, retiring from public life in 1999 at the age of eighty. At the African National Congress meeting held in December 1997, President Mandela confirmed this by stepping down as party leader. At that same meeting, Thabo Mbeki became the ANC party leader. As head of the biggest political group in the country, he is widely expected to become South Africa's second democratically elected president in 1999. This orderly transition is the great success of the new South Africa. In most African countries, the first election is usually the last one considered free and fair. There is a saying about such elections in Africa: "One man, one vote, one time." South Africa represents a major break from that sad history.

Opposite: **A mobile health clinic**

In 1999, some South African historical groups will commemorate the 100th anniversary of the Anglo-Boer War.

But on the lighter side, South Africa will host the All-Africa games in 1999, just a few years after it made its first appearance at the games. The Cape to Rio race, run every three years, will return in 1999 for the treacherous course across the Atlantic Ocean.

For teenagers in South Africa today, the changes have been the most dramatic. Their lives, more than most, reflect the difference between growing up under apartheid and growing up in a free society.

Stacey Augustine lives in the Coloured area known as Kensington. Under apartheid, she says, "There was no freedom. People were told what they couldn't do, where they couldn't eat. Other people were controlling your life." Now, she says, "I think of myself as a South African. The color of your skin has nothing to do with what you really are." For Stacey, who was seven years old when Nelson Mandela walked out of prison, apartheid is history.

White teenager Caryn Oosthuizen has seen the flow of Coloured and black children into her school. "They think the schools are better and now you can choose to go anywhere you want." Those children often come from inferior primary schools and need to catch up. Caryn does not expect to sacrifice her own education while that happens. "If the quality of education at the school goes down, I will change to Rustenburg girls' school."

South African teenagers Caryn Oosthuizen (right) and her friend Lindsay Pursch

National Holidays	
New Year's Day	January 1
Human Rights Day	March 21
Good Friday	varies
Family Day	March 31
Freedom Day	April 27
Workers' Day	May 1
Youth Day	June 16
National Women's Day	August 9
Heritage Day	September 24
Day of Reconciliation	December 16
Christmas Day	December 25
Day of Goodwill	December 26

Sharon Radebe grew up in Soweto, but when she was sixteen years old, her parents bought a house in a formerly white suburb of Johannesburg. It was just at the time when the laws were changing. Sharon is nostalgic for Soweto. In the beautiful area where she lives, she sees no one walking around. "I miss the people. It's so dead here. It's very different growing up in Soweto. You are with your friends. It's very different with the way the white children grow up."

Sixteen-year-old Nonkululeko Sibeko, who was born in Port Elizabeth, near the Ciskei, spoke only Xhosa for her first six years. After a few terrifying weeks in a poor, black school in a suburb of Cape Town, her parents moved her to an English school. "I was terrified at first but I learned English in three months."

"My parents told me a bit about apartheid. My mom was a lecturer at University of the Western Cape. Now she helps the parliamentarians to read the documents they have to work on. My dad is a high school teacher. He teaches Xhosa and history. Opportunities are amazing now. Now you can do anything you want to."

The ultimate reality of South Africa's future is likely to be a continuation of its present: most of the political power is in the hands of the black majority but most of the wealth remains in the hands of the white minority. New alliances between blacks and whites, such as the creation of a new political party by Bantu Holmisa, formerly of the ANC, and Roelf Meyer, formerly of the National Party, in 1997, will help keep South Africa truly democratic. Once shunned because of its racial policies, South Africa has become a mediator in regional disputes. It is poised to be the leader of the African continent.

Sharon Radebe

Timeline

World History

c. **2500** B.C. Egyptians build the Pyramids and Sphinx in Giza.

563 B.C. Buddha is born in India.

South African History

More than 2,000 years ago Bushmen live in what is now South Africa. **c.100** B.C.

Before A.D. 300, Bantu-speaking Africans migrate into territory of South Africa. **A.D. 300**

Iron Age settlements are established. **c.1000**

A.D. **313** The Roman emperor Constantine recognizes Christianity.

610 The prophet Muhammad begins preaching a new religion called Islam.

1054 The Eastern (Orthodox) and Western (Roman) Churches break apart.

1066 William the Conqueror defeats the English in the Battle of Hastings.

1095 Pope Urban II proclaims the First Crusade.

1215 King John seals the Magna Carta.

1300s The Renaissance begins in Italy.

1347 The Black Death sweeps through Europe.

1453 Ottoman Turks capture Constantinople, conquering the Byzantine Empire.

1492 Columbus arrives in North America.

1500s The Reformation leads to the birth of Protestantism.

Bartolomeu Dias reaches South African coast. **1488**

Settlers build stone houses and walls. **c.1500**

Jan van Riebeeck arrives from Holland. **1652**

1776 The Declaration of Independence is signed

1789 The French Revolution begins.

British take over Cape Colony from Dutch. **1806**

Shaka and Zulus conquer land and people. **1820**

Boers make Great Trek away from the Cape. **1836–1838**

Boers defeat Zulus at Battle of Blood River. **1838**

Diamonds are discovered. **1866**

Zulus defeat British at Battle of Isandhlwana. **1879**

British and Boer armies fight Africans. **1870–1880**

Gold is discovered. **1886**

1865 The American Civil War ends.

South African History

The Anglo-Boer War is fought.	1899– 1902
Union of South Africa is created from British colonies and Boer republics.	1910
African National Congress is founded.	1912
Natives Land Act is passed, restricting African ownership of land to "homelands."	1913
Nelson Mandela is born.	1918
National Party wins election and establishes policy of apartheid.	1948
Congress of the People write Freedom Charter.	1955– 1956
Police kill 69 black people at peaceful protest against pass laws. ANC and PAC are banned.	1960
ANC establishes Umkhonto we Sizwe (Spear of the Nation), and armed struggle against apartheid begins.	1961
Nelson Mandela is sentenced to life in prison.	1964
Students in Soweto protest use of Afrikaans in schools; about 1,000 are killed during the next 18 months.	1976
Steve Biko dies in police custody.	1977
State of Emergency is declared.	1985
State of Emergency is renewed.	1985
Ban on ANC and PAC is lifted by de Klerk. Mandela is freed after 27 years in prison.	1990
Apartheid is abolished.	1991
Chris Hani is assassinated. Nobel Peace Prize is awarded jointly to Nelson Mandela and F. W. de Klerk.	1993
First democratic elections are held. Nelson Mandela becomes president.	1994
Constitution guaranteeing rights for all is accepted and becomes law.	1996

World History

1914	World War I breaks out.
1917	The Bolshevik Revolution brings Communism to Russia.
1929	Worldwide economic depression begins.
1939	World War II begins, following the German invasion of Poland.
1950	The Korean War starts.
1957	The Vietnam War starts.
1963	President is Kennedy assassinated.
1969	Woodstock Rock Festival takes place.
1974	President Nixon resigns.
1989	The Berlin Wall is torn down, as Communism crumbles in Eastern Europe.
1990	The Persian Gulf War begins.
1996	Bill Clinton is reelected U.S. president.

Fast Facts

Zulu beehive huts

Official name: Republic of South Africa

Capital: Cape Town

Official languages: Sepedi, Sesotho, Setswana, siSwati, Tshivenda, Xitsonga, Afrikaans, English, isiNdebele, isiXhosa and isiZulu

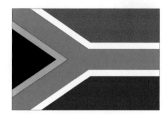

Flag of South Africa

Official religion: None

National anthem: *"Nkosi Sikelel' iAfrika"* meaning "God Bless Africa"

Government: Democratic, multiparty republic with two houses in parliament, one national and one provincial

Head of state and government: President

Area and dimensions: 472,281 square miles (1,223,201 sq km); measures irregular shape nearly 1,000 miles (1,600 km) both north to south and east to west

Bordering countries: Mozambique along northeast, Swaziland, Lesotho (surrounded by South Africa in the center east), Botswana, and Zimbabwe to the north, Namibia in the northwest. The west, south, and southeast borders are formed by Atlantic and Indian Oceans.

Highest elevation: Injasuti (peak), 11,181 feet (3,408 m) on border with Lesotho, in Drakensberg Mountains

Lowest elevation: Sea level along west, south, and east coastlines

Average temperatures:

	July (winter)	*January* (summer)
Cape Town	54°F (12.2°C)	70°F (20.9°C)
Kimberley	52°F (10.8°C)	78°F (25.3°C)
Johannesburg	51°F (10.4°C)	68°F (20.1°C)

Average temperature ranges from a mean of 73°F (23°C) in the north to 54°F (12°C) in the south and east.

Average annual rainfall: From more than 40 inches (100 cm) in the Drakensbergs and coast of Natal to less than 8 inches (20 cm) per year in Cape Town. Rainfall occurs mostly in the wintertime in Cape Town.

National population: Figures from a census taken in 1996 proved to be very surprising since they claimed there were only 37.9 million people in the country. Yet estimates in 1995 put the total at 41 to 43.5 million. It is not clear whether these figures include the illegal immigrants whose numbers are generally thought to be 4 to 5 million.

In the recent past, census figures for the black townships were not based on actual counts but by flying over the area and counting houses. Then estimates were made based on the number of people believed to be living in each house. The new census figures are based on door-to-door interviews conducted over a month-long period. However, since so many people in South Africa don't actually have a "door," it is likely that millions were simply not counted.

Historical population statistics:	
1970	22,783,000
1980	29,208,000
1985	33,198,000
1995	41,244,000
1996	37,859,000

In the past it was believed the population has been growing at about 2.4 to 2.5% annually. Rates range from 1.2% for whites to 2.7% for blacks. However, these figures are now changing because it is believed the rate for blacks is lower.

Projected population in 2000 based on the 1995 figures would be 46,663,740. If an estimated 4 million illegal immigrants are added in, the population of South Africa would be more than 50 million. This is considered by many people to be a reasonable estimate.

JOHANNESBURG

Population of largest cities in South Africa: (1995 estimate)

These figures cover only the central area of each city center:

Johannesburg	712,507
Pretoria	525,583
Cape Town	854,000
Durban	715,670
Port Elizabeth	303,353

Provinces and capitals:

Province	Capital
Gauteng	Johannesburg
Northern Province	Pietersburg
Mphumalanga	Nelspruit
Free State	Bloemfontein
KwaZulu-Natal	Pietermaritzburg
Eastern Cape	King Williams Town
Western Cape	Cape Town
Northern Cape	Kimberley
North-West	Mmabatho

Famous landmarks:

Voortrekker Monument in Pretoria was built in 1949 to commemorate the Battle of 1838.

Rhodes Memorial (left) is a dramatic statue of Cecil Rhodes on horseback overlooking Cape Town.

Taalmonument, Paarl, is an Afrikaner-designed language monument. A soaring spire represents the Afrikaans language and little mounds represent the black languages.

Shaka Monument, Stanger, is on the north coast of KwaZulu-Natal. This stone monument marks the site where Shaka had his military kraal (village).

The Big Hole is the site of a major diamond find at Kimberley.

Table Mountain is the enormous, flat-topped mountain at Cape Town.

Industry: Although South Africa's economy was built on gold and diamond mining, its economy is varied. It has a full range of manufacturing companies as well as the best ports in all of southern Africa. Agriculture accounts for less than 5% of its production. Beer is a major export. South Africa is the tenth largest producer of weapons in the world.

Currency: The South African rand is worth about $.20 in U.S. currency. Bills vary in size according to their value. Each rand is divided into 100 cents.

Weights and measures: Metric system

Literacy: *1990 by race:* Whites: 99%; Asians: 69%; Coloureds: 62%; Africans: 50%

Common South African words:

Afrikaans	a language that developed in South Africa among Dutch descendants; also spoken by most Coloureds
Afrikaner	a white person, usually of Dutch or German ancestry
Asian	a person whose ancestors came from India
biltong	dried meat
boer	a farmer, often used to describe an Afrikaner
boerewors	a sausage made by Afrikaners
Coloured	a person of mixed race
E'goli	a Zulu word meaning "place of gold," which is what Zulus call Johannesburg
mealies	roasted corn

To Find Out More

Nonfiction

▶ *Illustrated History of South Africa,* 3rd ed., Cape Town: Reader's Digest, 1994.

▶ Mallaby, Sebastian. *After Apartheid.* London: Faber and Faber, 1993.

▶ Pratt, Paula Bryant. *The End of Apartheid in South Africa.* San Diego: Lucent Books, 1995.

Biography

▶ Denenberg, Barry. *Nelson Mandela, No Easy Walk to Freedom.* New York: Scholastic, 1995.

▶ Mandela, Nelson. *Long Walk to Freedom.* Boston: Little, Brown & Co., 1995.

▶ Mandela, Nelson. *Mandela, An Illustrated Autobiography.* Boston: Little, Brown & Co., 1996.

Websites

▶ **South Africa Tourism Board**
http://www.africa.com

▶ **African National Congress**
http://www.anc.org.za/sanet.html

▶ **South Africa Online**
http://www.Southafrica.co.za

▶ **Mail & Guardian**
http://www.mg.co.za

▶ **Nelson Mandela's Children's Fund**
http://web.co.za/mandela/children

Index

Page numbers in *italics* indicate illustrations

A

African National Congress. *See* ANC (African National Congress).

Afrikaans language, 11–12

Afrikaners (People of Africa), 36–40, 44

Andries Pretorius, 39

   British people and, 42–43

   South Africa Republic, 40

   World War II and, 44, 46

   Zulu people and, 39

Afrikaners' National Party, 46

   agriculture, *24*, 71, 74–77, *74*, *76*

   map, *28*

   Niassa, 76–77

   ostrich farms, 76

   winemaking, 74–75, *74*

AIDS infections, 122

ANC (African National Congress), 44, 47–48, *47*, 123

Anglo-Boer war, 43, 124

animal life, 29–31

   rhinos, 30, *30*

   springbok, 31, *31*

   whales, 31, *33*

   wildlife reserves, 29, 32

apartheid, 11–15, *12*, *13*, *44*, *45*, 45–48, 54, 90

   banning (as form of punishment), 48

   F. W. de Klerk, President of South Africa, and, 53, *53*

   District Six, 49, *49*

   Dutch Reformed Church and, 93–94

   exiles, 50

   Hendrik Verwoerd, Prime Minister of South Africa and, 46–47

   Holy Bible and, 11

   homelands, 13

   literature and, 108

   passbooks, 13, *13*, 45

   South African police and, *51*

   spaza shops, 81

   townships, 12–13, 44, 67

art, 115

   Bushmen paintings, *23*

   District Six, 115

   South African National Gallery, 115

   Willie Bester, 115

Augustine, Stacey, 125

AWB, 63–64

B

banning (as form of punishment), 48

Barnard, Christiaan, 122

Bester, Willie, 115

Biko, Steve, 50, *50*

   murder of, 51, 65

Bill of Rights, 56, 58

biltong (food), 118

Black Consciousness Movement, 50

Blood River, 39

bobotie (food), 118

boerewors (food), 118

Boers. *See* Afrikaners (People of Africa).

Boesak, Rev. Allan, 95, *95*

Boraine, Alex, 64–65

Botha, P.W., Prime Minister of South Africa, 51–52, *51*
braais, 118, *118*
British Commonwealth of Nations, 48
British people
    Afrikaners and, 42–43
    Anglo–Boer war, 43
    cattle–killing disaster, 42
    Xhosa people and, 41–42
Bushmen, 24
    Drakensberg cave paintings, *23*, 24
Buthelezi, Mangosuthu, 60, *61*
    as Minister of Home Affairs, 61

C

Calvin, John, 93–94
Cape Agulhas, 19
Cape of Good Hope, 19
Cape to Rio yacht race, 106, *106*, 124
Cape Town, 19, *19*, *37*, *38*, 43
Cape to Rio yacht race, 106, *106*, 124
    District Six, 49, *49*
    South African National Gallery, 115
    Table Mountain, *22*, *22*
cattle-killing disaster, 42
cellular phone industry, 78, *78*
chromium mining, 69
cities
Cape Town, 19, *19*, *43*
    Durban, 26, *26*, 83, *83*
    Johannesburg, 27, *27*
    Sun City, 74, *74*
Clegg, Johnny, 109, *109*
climate, 21, 29
coastlines, 18–19, 28
currents, 19
Coloureds' Carnival, 112, *112–113*
Constitutional Assembly, 56
constitution, 56, 68
    official languages, 85
    temporary, 55
crime, 80

cultural tourism, 72–74, *73*
culture, 100–115
    art, 115
    foods, 118
    Klop Klop, *101*
    literature, 108–109
    maids, 119
    music, 110–111, *110–111*
    national holidays, 126
    plays, 108
    radio, 111–112
    sports, 101–108
    television, 89, *89*
    traveling circuses, 113
currency, 75, *75*
customary law, 62

D

de Klerk, F.W., President of South Africa, 53, *53*
diamond mining, 40, *40*, 69–70, *70*
    Big Hole at Kimberly, *40*
Dias, Bartolomeu, 34
District Six, 49, *49*, 108, 115
Drakensberg mountain range, 23–24, *24*, 39
    Bushmen paintings, *23*, 24
    Great Trek, 39, 64, 90
Durban, 26, *26*, 83, *83*
Dutch Reformed Church, 93–95

E

economy, 66–68, 71–72, 74–79, 81–83
    agriculture, 71, 74–77, *74*, *76*
    currency, 75, *75*
    hawkers (sidewalk vendors), 81, *82*
    international investment, 78–79, *79*, 81
    manufacturing, 71
    mining, 69–71
    security industry, 80
    Self--Employed Women's Union, 82
    service industry, *71*
    spaza shops, 81
    telephone companies, 78

Telkom, 73
tourism, 73
window dressing, 71
education, 16, *16*
school integration, 72
elections, 9, 15, *55*, 56, *56*, 124
voting rights, 15, 43, 55, *55*
exiles, 50

F
flag, 63, *63*
foods, 118
biltong, 118
bobotie, 118
boerewors, 118
braais, 118, *118*
mealie pap, 118
foreign investment. *See* international investment.
Furse, Elizabeth, 50

G
Gama, Vasco de, 28, *28*
geography, 18–24
coastline, 18–19, 28
Drakensberg mountain range, 23–24, *24*, 39
land borders, 20
map, *10*
geopolitical map, *10*
gold mining, 42, 69–70
Gordimer, Nadine, 108–109, *108*
government, 11
African National Congress, 44, 47
ANC (African National Congress), 44, 47–48, *47*, 123
Bill of Rights, 56, 58
constitution, 55–56, 68, 85
Constitutional Assembly, 56
customary law, 62
elections, 9, 15, *55*, 56, *56*, 124
end of apartheid and, 54
Nelson Mandela and, 9

PAC (Pan Africanist Congress), 47–48
Parliament, 56, 58–59, 62–63
separation of church and state, 93
traditional leaders, 62
Great Trek, 39, 90
AWB reenactment of, 63–64
Grey Street Mosque, 96

H
Hani, Chris, 14, *14*
hawkers (sidewalk vendors), 81, *82*
health care, 121–122, *122*
AIDS infections, 122
heart transplants, 122
tuberculosis infections, 122
heart transplants, 122
Heyns, Penny, 102, *103*
Hindu religion, 98, 99
Hluhluwe-Umfolozi Game Reserve, 33, *33*
holidays. *See* national holidays.
Holmisa, Bantu, 127
homelands, 13
housing, *67*
constitution and, 68
Mandela Village, 68, *68*
modern, 117, *117*
townships, 12–13, 44, 67
Hout Bay, 68

I
immigrants, 16
mining and, 70
Inkatha, 60
international investments, 78–79, *79*, 81
IsiXhosa language, 86

J
Johannesburg, 27, *27*
Johnnies Industrial Corporation, 77
Judaism, 98
Juluka, 109, *109*
July's People, 108–109

K

Karroo Desert, *21*
Khoikhoi people, 36
Klop Klop, *101*
Kramer, David, 108
Kruger National Park, 32–33, *32, 33*
KwaZulu–Natal, 28, 60–61, 76

L

Ladysmith Black Mambazo, 110–111, *110–111*
land borders, 20
Langlaagte farm, 42
languages, 84–85, 87–89
    Afrikaans, 11–12
    constitution and, 85
    Gustav Preller and, 88, *88*
    IsiXhosa, 86
    Nguni, 87
    SiSwati, 88
    Sotho-Tswana, 87–88
Lekganyane, Engenas, 91
literature, 108–109
    apartheid and, 108
    Nadine Gordimer, 108–109, *108*

M

Machel, Graca, 123
Mandela, Nelson, 8, 9, 12, *54, 57, 58,* 114
    constitution and, 58, *58*
    education of, 12
    Graca Machel and, 65, *65,* 123
    imprisonment of, 11
    Oliver Tambo and, 57
    as President of South Africa, 9, 11, 57
    private life of, 123
    release from prison, 53
    Winnie Mandela and, 123, *123*
Mandela Village, 69
Mandela, Winnie, *124*
manufacturing, 71
maps
    agricultural, 28

European expansion, 37
    geopolitical, *10*
    resources, *25*
    topographical, *21*
Maputo Corridor, 83
Maree, Sydney, *102*
Mbeki, Thabo, 14, 50, *124*
Mchunu, Sipho, 109
mealie pap (food), 118
Meyer, Elana, 102, *103*
Meyer, Roelf, 127
military, 82
mining, 69, 71, 77
    chromium, 69
    diamond, 40, *40,* 69–70, *70*
    gold, 42, 69–70
    migratory labor in, 70
    NUM (National Organization of
        Mineworkers), 77
    platinum, 69
Mtolo, Willie, 107, *107*
music, 109–111
    Juluka, 109, *109*
    Ladysmith Black Mambazo, 110–111,
        110–111
    Paul Simon, 111, *111*
Muslim religion, 96–98
Myer, Elana, 102, *103*

N

national anthem, 64
National Assembly, 59
National Council of Provinces, 59
national holidays, 126
National Union of Mineworkers. *See* NUM
    (National Union of Mineworkers).
Natives' Land Act, 44
Naudé, Rev. Beyers, 94
Ncome River, battle at, 39
Nguni language, 87
Niassa, 76–77
NUM (National Union of Mineworkers), 77

O

Olympic Games, 101–102, 107–108
    Atlanta Centenary Games, 102
    Elana Meyer, 102
    Willie Motolo, 107, *107*
Oosthuizen, Caryn, *125*, 125

P

PAC (Pan Africanist Congress), 47–48
PAGAD (People Against Drugs and
        Gangsterism), 97–98
Pan Africanist Congress. *See* PAC (Pan
        Africanist Congress).
Parliament, 59, 63
passbooks, 13, *13*, 45, *45*
people. *See also* culture.
    Afrikaners (People of Africa), 36–40, 43–
        44, 46
    British, 41–43
    Khoikhoi, 36
    San, 36
    Swazi, 88
    teenagers, 119, 121, *121*, 125, *125*
    Xhosa, 37, 86, *86*
    Zulu, 25, 28, 38–39, *38*, 60, *60*, 62, *73*, 92,
        92, 110, *110*
People Against Drugs and Gangsterism. *See*
        PAGAD (People Against Drugs and
        Gangsterism).
People of Africa. *See* Afrikaners.
Petersen, Taliep, 108
plant life, 29, *32*
protea, 31, *31*
platinum mining, 69
plays, 108
Preller, Gustav, 88, *88*
Pretorius, Andries, 39
protea, 31, *31*
Pursch, Lindsay, *125*

R

Radebe, Sharon, 126
radio, 111–112

Radio Show exhibit, 112
Ramaphosa, Cyril, 77, *77*
Raves, 119–121
religion, 90–99
    Dutch Reformed Church, 93–94, *94*
    Engenas Lekganyane and, 91
    Grey Street Mosque, *96*
    Hinduism, 98, 99
    John Calvin and, 93–94
    Judaism, 98
    Muslim, 96–98
racism and, 11
    sangomas, 92–93, *92*
    separation of church and state, 93
    Zion Christian Church, 91
resource map, *25*
rhinos, 30, *30*
Rhodes, Cecil, 41, *41*
Riebeeck, Jan van, 35–36, *35*
Robben Island, 8, 22, 114, *114*
Rorke's Drift battlefield, 25
rugby, 104–105, *104*

S

San people. *See* Bushmen.
sangomas, 92–93, *92*
SASO (South African Students
        Organization), 50
Scientific Committee on Antarctic Research,
        82
security industry, 80
Self-Employed Women's Union, 82
service industry, *71*
Shabalala, Joseph, 110
Shaka, chief of Zulu people, 38, *38*
Shaka Zulu, 73, *73*
Sharpeville Massacre, 45, *45*
Sibeko, Nonkululeko, 126
sidewalk vendors. *See* hawkers.
Simon, Paul, 111, *111*
SiSwati language, 88
soccer, 105, *105*
Sontonga, Enoch, 64

Sotho–Tswana language, 87–88
South Africa Republic, 40
South African Defense Forces, 82
South African National Gallery, 115
South African Navy, 82
South African Students Organization. *See* SASO (South African Students Organization).
spaza shops, 81
sports, 101–108
    All-Africa games, 124
    Cape to Rio yacht race, 106, *106*, 124
    Elana Meyer, 102, *103*
    Josia Thugwane, 102, *102*
    Mark Williams, 105
    Olympic Games, 102, 107–108
    Penny Heyns, 102, *103*
    rugby, 104–105, *104*
soccer, 105, *105*
Sydney Maree, *102*
    Willie Mtolo, 107
    World Rugby Cup competition, 104
springbok, 31, *31*
St. Lucia Wetlands, 77
Sun City, 74, *74*
Swazi people, 88

T–U
Table Mountain, 22, *22*
Tambo, Oliver, 14, *14*
    Nelson Mandela and, 57
teenagers, 121, *121*, 125, *125*
    Raves, 119–121
television, 89, *89*
Telkom, 73
Terre'Blanche, Eugene, 62–64, *62*
Thugwane, Josia, 102, *102*
topographical map, *21*
tourism, 72–74, *73*
townships, 12–13, 44, 67
traditional leaders, 62
Transkei Express, 86
traveling circuses, 113

Truth and Reconciliation Commission, 64–65
Tswana language, 87–88
tuberculosis infections, 122
Tutu, Desmond, Archbishop, 64–65, 93, *93*

U
Union of South Africa, 43–44

V
Valley of the Waves resort, *74*
Verwoerd, Hendrik, Prime Minister of South Africa, 46–47
Victor Verster prison, 8
Voortrekker Monument, 39, *39*
voting rights, 15, 43, 55, *55*

W
whales, 31
wildlife reserves, 29–30, *29*, 32
    Hluhluwe-Umfolozi Game Reserve, 33, *33*
    Kruger National Park, 32–33, *32*, *33*
Williams, Mark, 105
window dressing, 71
winemaking, 74–75, *74*
Witwatersrand region, 42
World Rugby Cup competition, 104
World War II, 44, 46

X
Xhosa people, 37, 86, 86
    British people and, 41–42

Z
Zulu people, 28, 60, *60*, 110, *110*
    Afrikaners and, 39
    battle with British, 25
    cultural tourism and, 72, 73
    Goodwill Zwelethini, King of, 62
    Mangosuthu Buthelezi, 60–61, *61*
    sangomas, 92, *92*
    Shaka, chief of Zulu people, 38, *38*
Zwelethini, Goodwill, King of Zulu people, 62

Meet the Authors

ETTAGALE BLAUER and JASON LAURÉ made their first trip to South Africa in 1977. They were inspired to go by the events of June 16, 1976, when students protested against use of Afrikaans in schools. They lived in the country for two years, traveling from coast to coast. They went into gold and diamond mines and talked to hundreds of people, especially teenagers. They also visited many of the sites described in this book including the Zulu battle sites. They spent four months in the Cape Province. After their book *South Africa, Coming of Age under Apartheid* was published in 1980, they were not permitted back into the country. They returned to South Africa for the first time in 1991 and were astonished at the changes they saw. "To see white, black, Asian, and Coloured people eating in the same restaurant, something so ordinary in most countries, but so extraordinary there, took my breath away," Ettagale Blauer says.

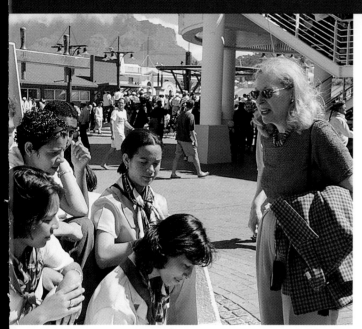

(above) **Ettagale Blauer talks to teens at Waterfront in Cape Town.**

(right) **Jason Lauré at election rally, Orlando Stadium, Soweto**

On many trips back since then, they have witnessed the elections, attended the swearing in of the first democratically elected Parliament, and seen the changes in the townships, the squatter camps, and the cities. They have watched businesses return to South Africa, and they have talked to friends whose cars were taken from them, friends whose sons were killed in the crime wave. They return to South Africa at least once a year to document the changes there.

Photo Credits